~ July 28, 20__

Chantel,

I wanted you to have a signed copy of my newest - #1 Best Seller!

I Hope you Enjoy It!

Your Friend,

DUI Defense:
The Down & Dirty DUI Defense Strategies That You Need To Know

By:
George F. McCranie IV, Esq.
Best Selling Author and Criminal Defense Attorney

ISBN: 978-0-9885523-7-1

For more information, please write:
We Published That, L.L.C.
c/o Adam Weart
PO Box 956669
Duluth, GA 30095

Dedication

I would like to thank my family and friends for all of their support and encouragement. Also, I would like to thank my staff, Team McCranie, for their continued support and dedication. But most of all, I would like to thank my wonderful wife, Danielle. She is the strong driving force that encourages me daily and has worked diligently to keep me on task and work to finish this book. This accomplishment, like so many others, would not be possible without my family's love, encouragement and support.

- George F. McCranie

Table Of Contents

Introduction

You probably never thought it would happen to you. As you were driving, a police officer pulled you over and accused you of drunk driving.

So you had a couple of drinks, but not many. You felt fine to drive home, but why did the officer stop you? Now what? What happens next? *How are you going to defend yourself?* Will you go to jail? Are you going to be fined *and put on probation? Is your picture going to be in the newspaper? Am I going to lose my job?* All of these questions are important, and you need answers!

Down and Dirty DUI Defense was written for people who have been stopped and accused of *Driving Under the Influence (DUI).* Being charged *with* DUI is *extremely* serious and can *have very* severe consequences *for you*, as well as an emotional and financial impact on your family.

Due to the rising number of deaths and injuries *"statistically"* related to DUI accidents, many states are imposing stiffer penalties for the offenders, in the state of Georgia, DUI is considered a **criminal** offense. *A DUI conviction will stay on your criminal record for the <u>rest of your life</u>.*

If you are convicted of DUI you could face jail time, a license suspension, *community service, pay for and complete a DUI risk reduction class (DUI school) and be required to serve 12 months on probation and have your picture printed in the newspaper!* Your car insurance will sky rocket and you can even lose your job! Having an experienced lawyer who can represent you is a *MUST*. A DUI is serious, and *your attorney should know* how to challenge *the* evidence that <u>*will be*</u> used against you!

Having represented and defended clients since 1998 that have been cited and arrested for DUI, I felt the need to write this book to educate people about *why they were arrested*, the possible consequences, and the importance and urgency of hiring *a qualified, competent and experienced DUI* attorney!

As a Driver, you need to remember that everything you *say* or *do will* be used against you *by the prosecutor.* That means if you *tell the officer that you have had* just one glass of wine *with dinner, or a couple of beers while watching the game* it will be *included* in the police officer's *incident* report. The Officer's report will often read – "Driver <u>admitted</u> to consuming alcohol". Whil*e getting out of your vehicle, if you use the door to pull yourself up because you have a bad back, the officer will make a note that you "had to use the door for support" or was unsteady and climbed out of the vehicle.*

It is important that you understand the reason for the *arrest* in the first place, as well as what to expect should you go to trial and have to defend yourself. When *an officer* stops *a suspected drinking driver* initially there were clues that *the officer noticed that aroused suspicion and caused* the officer *to turn on the blue lights and stop you.* When that happens, it is important to know <u>what to do</u> and <u>how to handle *yourself* in a way that will improve your chance of a successful outcome in this dreaded situation.</u>

There are 3 Phases *involved in* a DUI *stop before you are arrested.* Each *of the 3 P*hases will be discussed in the upcoming chapters.

Phase I will be discussed *in detail* in Chapter 1. In this chapter you will learn what prompted *the* officer to pull you over while driving. Just your driving behavior alone can send signals to other drivers, as well as to a police officer, that you *could be* intoxicated. Chapter 1 will shed some light on these types of driving *behaviors and what the officer is looking for.*

Personal contact with the *officer* is Phase II. When you are pulled over by an officer, your personal behavior will be *observed. Your* reactions to questions will be *noted by the officer in his detailed report.* Chapter Two will *educate* you on what *the officers look for* and how your *responses and reactions* can trigger more suspicion of *intoxication which can lead to your arrest.*

When you are pulled over for a DUI the contents of your vehicle will be examined *by law enforcement.* These contents can *and will* be used against you. In Chapter Three, you will learn *the types of items* to be aware of having in your vehicle that can be used against you *by the prosecutor.*

Phase III is the field sobriety tests. When a person is pulled over for a DUI, there are many types of tests that *officers give suspected drinking drivers. Some of these tests are simply made up by the officer. Some have been used in DUI cases but have no credible research to validate their usefulness in a DUI situation.* In Georgia, there are 3 approved Standardized Field Sobriety Tests. *These approved field sobriety tests* are voluntary. These tests will be discussed in Chapter 3. You will learn how you should handle yourself *if you decide to perform these standardized* tests *while* being under observation *by the officer.*

Chapter 4 will educate you about the most common form of DUI testing the Breath Test! Georgia currently uses the Intoxilyzer 5000 manufactured by CMI - a Kentucky based company. The 1970's based technology of the Intoxilyzer 5000 leaves much to be desired and will soon be replaced by a more modern machine.

Chapter 5 will educate you on what to expect when you are accused of DUI. It will also show you the importance of working with your attorney and what the attorney *should* expect from you. There are two types of trials *available in a DUI case in Georgia.* As you read Chapter 5, you will learn what they are, *and which one is better for you.*

After you finish reading Down And Dirty DUI Defense, I want you to understand what to expect if you were arrested for DUI *and what you need to do to improve your chances of winning your case.* You will also learn the importance of fighting for your rights *and not simply rolling over and letting the system manipulate you into pleading guilty to DUI. Remember, having* the right *DUI* defense team on your side can help you *successfully fight the charge and avoid all of the unpleasantness and public humiliation of a DUI conviction. This book is a compilation of notes my staff have made of actual client interviews I have had over the past 15 years. Many of the examples used in the book are loosely based on these events.*

CHAPTER 1 - Phase 1: Your Driving Behavior is Being Observed

Over the past 20 years there have been numerous *changes in the* DUI laws. *Most of these changes are* not in favor of a *drinking* driver and in fact - the laws are getting stiffer. The *legal drinking* age in all *50* states is now 21 years old.

In the United States statistics show drinking and driving accounts for a large number of alcohol-related accidents and deaths. Because of this, many states are *pushing for* more felony *statutes* and extended jail time *for* those who have been found guilty *of DUI related offenses.*

What happens when a driver has consumed alcohol? When a person *consumes* alcohol, it slows down the *brains function* by acting as a depressant. Your *muscle reaction time slows because of the delayed* messages *sent by* your brain. When a person who has been drinking is driving, his or her senses, reflexes *and responses* are *slowed to varying degrees.* For example: if a car in front of you stops, unexpectedly, you <u>may</u> not respond as quickly as *necessary to safely* stop your vehicle before striking the other car. When *a significant amount of* alcohol is present in *a persons system,* it can *cause the person to have* a distorted picture *of* reality. They may think they are *driving* in a straight line when in fact they are weaving *the car down the highway.* Or they think they are walking *and standing normally but* in actuality they are staggering *or swaying.*

Dangers of Driving While Drinking to Excess

If you are driving *unsafely* as a result of consuming alcohol *to excess*, you can be arrested for *DUI.* In Georgia, (where I practice) if you take the State's official chemical sobriety tests *(blood, breath or urine)* and the results indicate that your blood alcohol content is .08 *grams* or higher, you will be charged for DUI, regardless of how *well* you are driving.

Some studies indicate that having a blood alcohol content of just .10 *grams*, which is slightly higher than the legal limit, puts you at a seven times greater risk of being involved in a *fatal accident*.

Before You are Pulled Over

A police officer or *state* patrol officer *in Georgia is trained not to* pull you over unless *they witness suspicious or dangerous driving behavior. However, I believe the recent financial hardships faced by government entities have led to an increase in vehicle stops for defective equipment, etc – tag light violation being a favorite equipment infraction – in my area of Georgia.*

Phase I: Vehicle in motion. There are cues an officer looks for prior to turning on the blue lights and pulling you over. Some of the cues an officer is taught to look *for* include:

1. **Weaving**. If you are weaving in your lane that is a cue.
2. **Weaving across lanes**. Anytime a driver is weaving (to the extreme) across the center line into the other lane is a red flag. *The best example I can give you of this cue is the recent public service commercials showing the truck with its cab filled with beer and the driver is weaving (severely) before being stopped at a roadblock.*
3. **Turning with a wide radius**. This adds suspicion and *was recently one of the top reasons for stopping a suspected drinking driver in the Metro Atlanta area.*
4. **Almost striking another object or vehicle**. This *cue indicates your reflexes, depth perception and reaction times could be slowed and you may be under the influence of alcohol or drugs.*
5. **Straddling the center or lane marker**. Straddling a lane or marker and not returning to the correct lane will raise a red

flag *and is a classic example of bad driving that attracts unwanted attention from law enforcement.*

6. **Appearing to be impaired.** If something appears to be wrong while driving, you will be pulled over. *A recent example of this involved a driver sitting at a red light and an officer noticed the driver's cigarette had burned all the way to the filter and was hanging from the drivers lip. The light turned green and the driver failed to react for over 10 seconds.*

7. **Driving on something other than a designated roadway**. Driving on the *shoulder of the road or in the emergency lane are examples of this cue that will draw immediate attention from an officer.*

8. **Driving into opposing or crossing traffic**. Not only is this dangerous, it is a cue *that the driver may be* distracted and slow to react *possibly due to excessive consumption of alcohol or use of drugs.*

9. **Slow response to traffic signals**. A delay in adhering to traffic signals can raise a red flag. *Remember the driver with the cigarette!*

10. **Turning abruptly or illegally.** Sudden impulsive moves, *changing lanes or turning without using a blinker* will raise a red flag. *This cue is sometimes used to give the officer reasonable articulable suspicion to stop a driver who turned before entering a roadblock.*

Video: DUI-What An Officer Looks for in Your Driving?

(Use QR Reader to watch video on your smart phone)

The Blue Lights *are* Flashing

As you have read the list of cues an officer is looking for, you are probably saying to yourself, "I do some of these things whether I have been drinking or not". That is probably true, but what you have to remember is - these are cues an officer will use in sizing up the situation. If you slip up and weave in your lane a couple of times and correct the situation, you may not get pulled over. But, if there are no changes in your erratic driving and more than one *cue* is observed, *the officer is trained to pull you over and investigate.*

Once the blue lights are turned on, and the officer is pulling you over, *it's important* to pay close attention to *your driving and how you are going to pull your vehicle safely to the side of the road.* The officer is trained to observe *your driving* after the blue lights *are turned on and use his observations against you in court.*

There are cues the officer is looking for *after the blue lights are activated*, such as:

1. **An attempt to flee**. This is **NOT** a good idea to try to outrun the *officer. Trying to outrun or hide from the officer is dangerous and* will only make the situation worse.
2. **No response to emergency equipment**. By not responding to *the officer's* emergency *lights and continuing to drive in complete disregard of the officer will certainly be noted in the incident report. In certain situations drivers have been charged with Fleeing and Attempting to Elude the officer for (As a husband and father of a teenage daughter, I have advised my family that in situations where they are unable to confirm the identity of the law enforcement vehicle that is attempting to pull them over - they should immediately call 911 and explain who and where they are and that they will proceed to a safe location and then stop for the "officer")* there have been numerous incidents where people have impersonated law enforcement officers in order to *victimize female drivers. I believe this is the safest and most reasonable reaction for a concerned driver to make in this potentially dangerous situation.*
3. **Slow response**. *Because excessive use of* alcohol and drugs *tend to* dull a person's senses, a slow response can be noted in the officer's report and used against you.
4. **An abrupt swerve**. The officer will observe how you are handling your vehicle and *an abrupt swerve will be noted as unsafe driving and included in the incident report.*
5. **Striking the curb or another object**. By striking the curb or another object, it *can* display your lack of *coordination and level of intoxication. This is also another classic example of an intoxicated driver.*

You might be surprised to learn that <u>speeding</u> by itself is <u>not</u> one of the *cues* that a driver is *drinking or under the influence.* Remember, *excessive consumption of alcohol dulls the senses and slows a driver's reaction times. It takes faster eye hand coordination and depth perception to safely operate a* *vehicle <u>above</u> the legal speed limit. So speeding <u>without</u> any other cue such as weaving or swerving should not lead the officer to suspect the driver is drinking.*

Video: DUI-Is Speeding a Cue to DUI?

Video: DUI-What Does the Officer Look for After Blue Lights are Turned On?

Your Initial Reaction

If you were at a bar or party and had some drinks and decided to drive yourself home, it is important that you know what an officer is looking for the minute you put your keys in the ignition.

You may have gotten behind the wheel after *a couple of* drinks and not *been stopped*, but there is always *a chance you will be stopped and suspected of being an intoxicated driver.* When you get behind the wheel of your vehicle, pay close attention to your driving. If you are stopped, the officer is going to be watching everything you do and listening to every word you say. Use caution to not make a bad situation worse! Being pulled over is just the beginning of *the officers observations of you and the end of Phase I. In my years of defending drinking drivers Phase II can often make or break a clients' defense.*

CHAPTER 2 - Phase II: Personal Contact with the Officer

Now that you have been singled out *because of your* driving or equipment violation and pulled over by an officer or stopped at a roadblock, you *should pay close attention to how you answer the officers' questions and respond to his instructions.* Remember, *the officer believes he has a reason to pull you over, and if you are suspected of drinking and driving, you should try very hard to act normally.* What you do during *Phase II, including your personal contact and interaction with the officer, can determine whether or not the officer decides to move on to Phase III – Standardized Field Sobriety Testing.*

Video: DUI-Examples of What is Not an Indicator of Drunken Driving

Phase II *is the officers' observation and personal contact with you after you have been stopped.* There are 28 cues that officers are looking for, which are taught under the National Highway Safety and Traffic Administration **(NHTSAA)** *training*

program which is used throughout the nation and by the State of Georgia.

The 28 cues are broken down into the following categories:

- **Things *the officer sees***
- **Things *the officer hears***
- **Things *the officer smells***

The initial questions the officer *asks* you can be determined by what he or she observed *of* your driving *and* what was initially observed as the officer approached the vehicle.

In Georgia, if you are pulled over and the officer asks you, "Have you been drinking?" And *your answer is*, "I had a couple of drinks/beers/glasses of wine/zanaxes earlier," rest assured, you will be getting out of the vehicle! You *will not only* have raised a red flag, *but you will have taken it and planted it squarely on the hood of your car with a sign on your forehead saying –ARREST ME!!!* In my experience listening to hundreds of clients tell me this exact answer to the question - *Without a doubt you are headed directly to Phase III and will be asked to take field sobriety tests!*

Your responses *and reactions* are going to cause you a lot of grief - if you don't know how to respond properly and *effectively*.

Let's set up Phase II with a scenario that is repeated literally a thousand times a year all over the state of Georgia and the nation. You just left the party/bar/girlfriends or boyfriends house/ buddies house/ family reunion/ finished cutting the grass/ been fishing or hunting/ or even just received a call from a family member or friend who needs you to come get them from jail because they have been arrested for DUI. (Believe it or not - the last example REALLY happens!) You've only had a couple of drinks/beers/glasses of wine etc. and you feel fine to drive. You're driving along without noticing any problems with your driving at all. Then out of the blue you see a license check (roadblock) ahead. Your driving is fine, no problems, there is nothing different about your driving from the two cars in front of you. You wait your turn, pull up to the checkpoint, stop and roll down your window……

I think the easiest way to explain Phase II is to give a brief summary of selected cues an officer will look for *if you are suspected of drinking and driving.*

THINGS THE OFFICER CAN SEE

As *soon as* the officer approaches and is able to get a clear view *of your vehicle, he is observing you! From your appearance, to the things you are doing before he even gets to your window, you ARE being watched. The officer is watching you try to find your registration or fumble to light a cigarette. He is watching to see if you try to hide a beer or drugs. He is watching to see if you try to change seats with a passenger. Bottom line – if you make any unusual moves in the vehicle, it can and will make the officer suspicious and it will be included in his report. When the officer starts asking you questions and giving you instructions the REAL observation begins. I have included some of the observations I have seen officers make time and again on DUI incident reports.*

- **Forgetting to produce documents**. When an officer approaches your vehicle and asks for your driver's license and vehicle registration, it is not unusual for a person who *has consumed an excessive amount of alcohol* to forget to provide *both of* the documents that the officer requests. The officer is trained to use questions and instructions that will divide your attention. *It is common practice for officers to use this strategy of dividing your attention in order to test if you can follow multiple instructions without becoming distracted.* Not being able to focus on *the officers' questions and instructions will* raise a red flag.

- **Producing the wrong documents**. An officer will ask you to produce specific documents. If you provide the wrong ones, it will raise a red flag. *Don't be the driver who hands the officer a credit card and gym membership card instead of their driver's license and vehicle registration. At the Motion to Suppress hearing or trial, you can bet the officer will gladly tell the Judge or jury about your "mistake"!*

- **Fumbling and dropping your wallet, purse or documents**. An intoxicated person may have trouble holding things and drop *things like* his or her wallet, purse or documents. *The officer is trained to look for these types of problems and will make sure that it is in the incident report.* Imagine the effect that this type of observation can have on a jury when the officer describes you as "unable to even hold your wallet"!

- **Is unable to retrieve documents using his or her fingertips**. *Officers are trained that* coordination and grasping objects can be a problem *for* an intoxicated person. An officer is going to watch how you retrieve the requested documents *(driver's license and vehicle registration)*, as well as observing how you hand them over.

- **Failing to see the documents**. When an officer asks you to produce a specific document, and it is visible to the officer but not you, that is problematic. *You may be very nervous and this may be the reason for your oversight. You can bet the officer will note in the incident report and testify in court that you should have been able to see the documents right in front of you if he could see them from outside the vehicle.* It raises a red flag with the officer and puts you under more suspicion *of being intoxicated.*

If you are nervous and you hear the officer comment about it, you should give your own explanation. Something as simple as having difficulty removing your drivers' license from your wallet can be used by the officer against you at trial. You know it was stuck because your wallet is full of credit cards. If you don't tell the officer why you had the problem, the video and audio system will not record your explanation of the real reason. Remember, you could be on video, and the officer should be wearing a microphone which records everything you and the officer say. Make sure to give your side of the story. It could make all of the difference to the judge or jury.

Video: DUI- What Does the Officer Look for After They've Stopped a Driver?

THINGS THE OFFICER HEARS

When an officer approaches you in your vehicle, he or she is going to ask you a lot of questions. Your answers to the questions and how quickly and accurately you answer them is very important. Remember your answer can and will be used against you. Examples of what an officer is listening for are:

Slurred Speech. When the officer begins asking questions, and he thinks your speech is slurred, you have a problem! It would be best if you remembered to explain to the officer you just left your dentist office and your mouth was numbed, otherwise it will trigger a red flag. The dentist example is, of course, only an example – if you had been to the dentist. Regardless of the reason the officer thinks you have slurred speech, you will be raising suspicion that you have been drinking or using drugs. Usually the officer is not familiar with a driver's normal speech pattern and speed. A thick Southern accent may seem like slurred speech to a Metro-Atlanta officer.

Admission of Drinking. One of the first questions you will be asked is "Have you been drinking?" As soon as you say something like "yes" or "only a couple earlier today", rest assured you will be given field sobriety tests. Of course you have been raised to answer questions truthfully, but in this situation it may be wise not to admit to consuming alcohol, regardless of the amount or time consumed. I advise my clients that it is best not to answer this question and start questioning the officer about your right to have an attorney present when you are being questioned. Sometimes this approach will surprise the officer and he will lose his cool -- on video!!!

Video: DUI-What Happens if I Admit to the Officer That I Have Been Drinking?

___*Inconsistent Responses*___. *As you begin answering the officer's questions and your answers are inconsistent and keep changing, a red flag will be raised. If you are asked where you are coming from and you say "My friends party, uh, house – I mean work." The chances of the officer asking you to submit to field sobriety tests just went through the roof!*

___*Unusual Statements*___. *If an officer asks you questions and you begin rambling on with answers that don't make sense or are unusual, a red flag will be raised. I have seen drivers asked the year model of their vehicle and give responses like – "It's pretty old, I really need a new one. Have you seen the new Chargers? Hey, isn't that a Charger you're driving? What kind of gas mileage does it get? Because mine is a gas hog!" This driver should have kept quiet because she got to ride in the officer's new Charger - in the back seat – straight to the local jail!!!*

___*Abusive Language*___. *Trying to keep yourself calm and composed can be difficult. If you use abusive language, not only will it tend to make the officer mad, but it doesn't sound good on the video. Remember, a judge or jury may get to see the video and the* *prosecutor will describe your cursing or derogatory comments as that of an out of control, abusive, disrespectful drunk! Law enforcement is trained to deal with abusive language and disrespectful comments. Many officers now take classes called "Verbal Judo" in order to best take advantage of this type of situation. Well trained officers will make your rantings look especially bad on the video and set you up to be the classic "abusive drunk" the judge or jury expects to see in a DUI case.*

Video: DUI-What Does the Officer Look for After Stopping a Driver?

Video: DUI-What Does the Officer Look for When you Get Out of Your Vehicle?

THINGS THE OFFICER SMELLS

As the officer approaches your vehicle, he is not only looking at your appearance and reaction to <u>his</u> questions and demands. He is also looking out for specific smells.

In most cases the smell *is coming from* you, your *vehicle or passengers. I've* listed *a few of the smells that officers are trained to notice.*

<u>Alcoholic beverages</u>. Open containers that have alcoholic beverages in them *give off* odors. Also, an alcoholic beverage that has spilled *on you, your passengers or in your vehicle* will give off odors. *It usually surprises my clients when I tell them that pure alcohol has <u>no smell</u> --- it's odorless! For those of you who grew up back in the 1980's with Michael Jackson, parachute pants and "Hammer Time" an example you may remember is the 180 proof alcohol called - Golden Grain. When I was a youth it was used to make the classic southern mixture called <u>Swamp Frog</u> or <u>Hunch</u>*

<u>Punch</u>. If you are as old as I am – think back -- you couldn't smell the alcohol in the mix! In fact, you don't smell alcohol in a beer or vodka drink. You smell what the drink (alcoholic beverage) is made <u>from</u>, or <u>flavored</u> <u>with</u>. In beer you smell the barley or hopps. The same goes for other types of alcoholic beverages such as scotch or rum.

Experienced and well trained officers make sure to note in their incident reports that they observed the smell of an "alcoholic beverage" coming from the vehicle or the person of the driver. Then they often clarify, after talking to the driver, that the odor of the alcoholic beverage was determined to be coming from the drivers' breath. If you have *recently consumed an alcoholic beverage and the officer smells it, most experienced officers will ask you more questions about your drinking such as where you had your first drink, time of first drink/last drink, type of alcoholic beverage, its size etc. If you get to this point, expect to be asked to perform <u>field sobriety tests</u>!*

Video: DUI-Does the Officer Really Smell Alcohol?

"Cover-Up" Odors. Do you really think its possible to hide *the odor of an alcoholic beverage* with gum, breath mints, perfume or cologne? *Many of my previous clients thought they could. Some have used breath strips, some mouthwash, even others believe in the camouflaging ability of the unusually strong breath mints that come in the little metal tin! I even had a client that accidentally drank --- wait for it ---- cologne!!! In my experience these attempts usually fail. In my client's experience with the cologne --- it really failed!!! Most people's breath doesn't normally smell like peppermint or in the extreme case* Polo *and the officer will be very suspicious*. If you are fumbling around trying to camouflage the smell, the officer will be on to you!

Marijuana. The smell of marijuana is very distinctive and easy to recognize. If you have been smoking a joint and/or any passengers have, the smell will be in your vehicle and clothing. *If the officer suspects the driver of smoking marijuana he is trained to request a blood test and not use the Intoxilyzer 5000 breath test. Books have been written on DUI and marijuana and how to defend the "smoking driver". The explanation and analysis of a DUI based on suspected drugs will have to be a topic for my future books - because it deserves a book of its own. But I will give you an interesting piece of info – the Georgia Bureau of Investigation (GBI) crime lab* does not test for the active *ingredient in marijuana –* THC. *The states test looks for the* non-active *metabolite of marijuana that is present in a smoker's blood after the THC is processed by the body. In other words, the governments test doesn't look for the chemical that* impairs *a driver – THC - it only looks for the non-impairing byproduct that remains in a smoker's blood and fatty tissues long after the active and impairing THC is gone!*

Other Unusual Odors. An officer, who has pulled you over for suspicion of DUI, has been trained to identify different smells or odors. If it's not the smell of alcohol or marijuana, but another suspicious smell is coming from you or your vehicle, you will be questioned. *Twenty years ago this unusual smell wouldn't have been relevant but today it is arguably the fastest growing addiction problem in the United States --- Methamphetamine (Meth). People* *have actually transported the volatile chemical - anhydrous ammonia - used to make meth in <u>open</u> 5 gallon containers, in their vehicles! Usually in the trunk, but also amazingly even in the back seat! Anhydrous ammonia is commonly used on farms as an agricultural chemical. Not only is this an extremely dangerous and stupid idea, but it also has a distinctive and nauseating smell that will be instantly recognizable to any <u>farmer</u> or <u>law enforcement officer</u>.*

How You Exit the Vehicle

After the officer has approached your vehicle and has made specific observations, he or she may ask you to exit your vehicle. Remember, the officer is watching you closely and monitoring your every move. Below are a few things an officer will watch for when *you exit* the vehicle.

Angry, Unusual Reactions. When asked to exit your vehicle, if you are angry and show unusual reactions to the officer's request, a red flag will be raised. *Throwing objects in the car and kicking the door open are <u>not</u> normal reactions to being asked to exit your vehicle. After getting out I do not suggest that you kick the door closed with such force that you break the window! Bad idea for a Driver I saw on videotape of a DUI stop! Not only does this type of behavior look and sound bad on video, but it can also act to change the "normal" stop into a situation where the officer believes his safety is in jeopardy. If your angry reaction is so over the top the officer believes he needs to use force to protect himself it is going to be a bad day for you! This is a very dangerous situation that you DO NOT want to be in.* Of course you are *angry and* upset, but anger triggers suspicion and fear, so watch your behavior.

Can't Follow Directions. If you are asked to exit your vehicle and can't follow the directions of the officer, this is suspicious behavior that can raise a red flag. *An example is, the officer tells you to step to the back of your car. You exit the car and then walk out into the road. The officer calls you back and you tell the officer you thought he wanted you to cross the road and stand on the sidewalk. OR -*

one of the examples that sticks out in my mind after practicing criminal defense law for 15 years, the driver opens the hood of the car and then takes the radiator cap off – scalding himself and sending a huge cloud of smoke boiling from under the hood! You can imagine how this looked on video. Not a case that most experienced DUI defense attorneys are lusting to take to trial. Remember, you should listen carefully to the instructions the officer gives you and act accordingly.

Leaves Car in Gear. *Believe it or not this really does happen. I've seen it not only in DUI cases but also in other regular traffic stops. Sometimes the extreme nervousness caused by being stopped by law enforcement in a public place and the stress from the resulting public humiliation, distracts a driver and they simply forget to put the vehicle in park. I've seen examples of all different types of drivers that simply forget to put the vehicle in park - teens, active duty military, city officials, truck drivers and even --- you guessed it.... police officers themselves!!! If you don't believe me – just go to* www.YOUTUBE.com *and search "Runaway Police Car". You will be amazed at the videos!!!*

Can't Open Door. Unless your car door is broken *or you drive a car that used to be on the classic TV show Dukes of Hazard (you know the old General Lee),* the officer is going to observe you opening the door. If you can't open it because you can't focus *or aren't coordinated enough to find the door handle* the officer should note it in his report. I've seen videos where the officer actually has to help the driver open the door. This type of situation doesn't look or sound good on video. Keep calm and act normally, or be prepared to explain your actions in court.

Uses Vehicle for Support. If you have exited your vehicle and keep your hand on the vehicle *or simply lean on it, the officer may believe that because of a high level of alcohol or drugs in your system you needed to use the vehicle for support. Sometimes drivers have back, leg or hip problems and they* need *to use the vehicle for support. Or some drivers are naturally relaxed and as their normal course of behavior will lean against the vehicle while the officer calls in their* *information etc. My standard advice is to act normal. If you would normally lean on the vehicle because of a medical condition, ask the officer if it is ok for you to lean on the car because of your bad back or knee etc. If you do this, you have effectively taken the argument away from the officer that you did it because you were intoxicated!*

What Not to Say

Using common sense when being pulled over by an officer is a must. Trying to make a bad situation better by attempting to *"talk your way out of it" usually only makes it worse for you.*

An example of making a *bad* situation worse would go something like this: the officer pulls you over and asks, "have you been drinking?" *Think about your response, the following examples <u>won't</u> help you and may make your defense <u>much</u>, <u>much</u> harder.*

"I've only had a couple of beers at my friends party and I haven't smoked weed since this morning"   *or*

"I haven't been drinking, but I just took some Xanax."

    or

"I've only had one drink, but I've taken my pain meds and all this other <u>prescription</u> medication. It's okay officer – I have the prescription bottles right here!"

These are not *answers that will help you "talk your way out of it". As a matter of fact, these are terrible answers!!! My standard advice is probably the same advice your mother has given you, "if you cannot say anything good, don't say anything at all!"*

At my office, my motto is, ***"Admit Nothing, Deny Everything, Demand Proof^{sm}!"***

Don't give law enforcement the information they need to successfully prosecute you! Many drivers talk themselves into jail. Don't let that be you! *My standing advice to clients about answering officer's questions that could hurt them in Court is ---- "don't answer any question that would require you to give an incriminating statement." This means if the question is, "have you been drinking tonight?" I would recommend a response such as:*

1. *"if you are going to ask me questions, can I call my attorney before I answer?"*

or

2. *"aren't you supposed to read me Miranda Warnings before you ask me questions?"*

or

3. *"am I in your custody or am I free to leave?"*

The point of your response is to not give an incriminating or incorrect answer to the question "have you been drinking tonight". You should know that the officer will most likely say that you – (1) can't call your attorney, (2) he doesn't have to read you Miranda Warnings and (3) you are in his custody and you are not free to leave. Legally many courts will agree with the officer, however, most jurors "know from TV" that you should be able to call an attorney and the police must read you Miranda Warnings if you are in their custody. (Many people are supposed to know that what happens on TV – isn't the way it works in real life!) Many times my client's best defense is

*keeping their mouths shut and not answering or volunteering
any incriminating statements!*

Video: Miranda-When are Miranda Rights Required?

Things That Can Be Used Against You

Contents of Your Car

Even the contents *of* your vehicle can be used against you *by
law enforcement and the prosecutor.* In South Georgia, there are
many *bumpy dirt* roads. *The amazing thing is that some people will
get pulled over with an open 12-pack or case of beer in the
passenger area of the vehicle!*

For example:

In the 12-pack, 3 are unopened and the remaining 9 open or
empty cans are <u>in</u> the *vehicle* laying in the floorboard, cup holder or
seat! I am not advocating littering, but don't leave the *empty* cans in

the *vehicle* if you have been drinking! When the officer
that *stopped* you asks, "have you been drinking?" and your response
is, "only a couple of *beer*," that is not going to fly if *they see* 9 empty
cans in the floorboard. Why should the officer believe you? *He has
the evidence that you have consumed 9 beers right in front of
him! I've seen many veteran officers then repeat back "so you've
only had a couple?" and then ask you to hand them all of the empty
cans in the passenger area. When you do they'll make comments
like "this one still is half full" or "this one is still cold" – you get the
picture. They do this not just to get the evidence but also for the
benefit of the VIDEO! They have just shown a judge or jury (via the
video) that you lied to them about the amount of alcohol you have
consumed. It is usually a downhill ride for the driver at court once
video evidence like this is shown. I want y'all to understand - I
agree with the old public service commercial where "Woodsey the
Owl" used to say, "Give a hoot – Don't pollute!"* Don't litter,
but dispose of any empty cans in the proper trash receptacle!! Don't
leave evidence in your car that can be used to prosecute you!!!

Never leave the following items in your car:

1. *Any* **open or empty alcohol container** – *beer cans, open
   liquor or wine bottles, etc.*
2. **Prescription pill bottles** – *often causes an officer to suspect
   a DUI based on prescription meds.*
3. **Cigarette** *packs or cigar boxes – many times these are used
   to conceal illegal drugs, etc.*
4. **Anything associated with illegal drugs or drug use** – *such
   as "roach clips", cigarette rolling papers, pipes, bent
   spoons, digital scales or jeweler's bags etc.*

If you have anything that *would* cause *an* officer to be suspicious and
indicates that you *could be* under the influence of drugs or
alcohol, *you are going to be asked to take field sobriety tests and will
most likely be arrested for DUI.*

By leaving items in the car that an officer can see *"in plain view"*, you are *providing law enforcement and the prosecutor valuable evidence to help them prosecute you!!!* Be smart and get rid of your trash.

CHAPTER 3 - Field Sobriety Test

You've been pulled over for any number of reasons that could include: weaving, failure to stop at a stop sign, turning with a wide radius, headlight violation, failure to use a turn signal or my favorite – a tag light violation! You've given the officer your driver's license, proof of insurance and registration, answered his questions and possibly admitted to drinking earlier.

Or you may have just driven up to a DUI/ license checkpoint/roadblock and the officer says he smells alcohol, saw an open container of an alcoholic beverage, you admitted to having a few drinks earlier or he saw prescription pill bottles in your vehicle etc. Now you are about to be asked to "step out of the vehicle" and "would you mind performing a few field sobriety tests?" You haven't just entered "The Twilight Zone" - but you are in a virtual - no win – situation! You aren't familiar with the tests, the test instructions or how to perform these tests - <u>and you don't get to practice</u>! Worst of all, some of the officer's observations he will include in his report <u>cannot be disproven by the video</u>!

Video: DUI-How Does the Officer's Video & Audio Work?

Because the officer *now believes he should request* field sobriety *tests*, things aren't looking too good for you. *The*

officer <u>won't</u> voluntarily tell you that these Standardized Field Sobriety Tests (SFST) are <u>completely voluntary</u>. He'll say something like, "Do you mind doing a few tests for me?" or "How about doing a couple of tests to show that you're ok to drive?" 95% of drivers will agree because they <u>think</u> they can pass these tests –
<u>Wrong</u>! Remember, they don't know what the tests are, how to take the tests, that they will be graded on their performance even before they are told to start the tests, what constitutes a mistake, how the tests are scored, what is a passing grade and they <u>will not be able to practice before</u> actually taking the tests! REMEMBER: ALL OF THE SFSTs ARE VOLUNTARY!!!

There are 3 approved *SFSTs* in Georgia – (not including the preliminary breath test (PBT) that many officers carry with them). *This portion of the book describing the SFSTs is NOT an exhaustive examination of these tests. It is designed to give the reader an introduction to this <u>extremely complicated and detailed topic</u>. An entire book could easily be dedicated to just one of the tests. In fact, there are many books and articles written on the subject of SFSTs that take on the topic in minute detail and with great scholarly precision. I have included an overview of each of the SFSTs approved for use in Georgia.* Here is a breakdown of the 3 *SFSTs approved for use in Georgia – they are listed in the <u>correct order</u> the officer should give them.*

Video: DUI-How Many Standardized Field Sobriety Tests are Approved by NHSTA?

1. Horizontal Gaze Nystagmus Test

The *Horizontal Gaze Nystagmus* (HGN) test involves the eyes. Nystagmus is an involuntary jerking or bouncing of the eyeball that occurs when there is a disturbance of the vestibular (inner ear) system or the oculomotor control of the eye. HGN refers to a lateral or horizontal jerking *of the eye* when the eye gazes to the side.

Alcohol consumption or consumption of certain other central nervous system depressants, inhalants or phencyclidine, can hinder the ability of the brain to correctly control eye muscles and *can* cause *the* jerking or bouncing that is associated with HGN.

As the degree of impairment becomes greater, the jerking or bouncing becomes more pronounced. An officer who is conducting the HGN test is going to check both eyes twice for *each clue to determine* if there is nystagmus present.

The HGN test requires an object to follow with your eyes *(stimulus)*, such as a pen, finger or the tip of a penlight. *The HGN test is the only one of the 3 tests that is a <u>scientific</u> test. As such, the HGN test must be administered by the officers EXACTLY as they are taught using the approved NHTSA instructions and procedures. If the officer fails to give the proper instructions to the driver or fails to administer the test correctly under the NHTSA guidelines, the results can be "suppressed" by the court and not presented as evidence.*

The *officer is trained to place the stimulus* 12 to 15 inches from your face and slightly higher than eye level. By placing an object *slightly* above eye level, it will open your eyes further and make *the* movement *of your eyes* easier *for the officer to* observe. *The stimulus should not be over the top of your head, only slightly above eye level.*

The officer will instruct you to follow the object with your eyes *and your eyes only.* <u>Your head should remain still.</u> *I find it amazing that many times the officer will list in their reports that the driver was "unsteady on their feet" or was "swaying" and will then proceed to administer the HGN test – remember the HGN REQUIRES the driver to keep their head still. This is what I call the famous "disappearing sway"! The driver had it before taking the HGN and had it after taking the HGN, but during the administration of the HGN –kept his head perfectly still!!! So the officer says he hasn't violating the rules when he administered the test!*

Once the object is positioned, the officer *should* check for signs of medical impairment. The officer *should* check for equal pupil size *and resting nystagmus.* The officer *should* check for "equal tracking" by moving the object quickly across your entire field of vision to see whether both of your eyes follow the object simultaneously. *The officer should then check each of your eyes for each "clue" twice.*

These are the standardized clues:

--Lack of Smooth Pursuit

--Distinct and Sustained Nystagmus at Maximum Deviation

--Onset of Nystagmus Prior to 45 degrees

This gives a total of 6 clues on the HGN, 2 for each eye. If a driver exhibits 4 or more clues on the HGN, the officer's training manual indicates that the blood alcohol content (BAC) is above 0.10. To learn more about the *HGN* test go to: http://www.nhtsa.gov/people/injury/enforce/nystagmus

There are several things to keep in mind about the HGN test. The test result is completely objective and based only on what the officer sees or believes he sees. The best DUI arrest video ever made will not be able to confirm OR refute what the officer says he saw! However, your DUI defense attorney should be able to use the video and/or the officer's testimony in court to prove the officer failed to give the proper instructions for the test or he failed to administer the HGN test correctly. REMEMBER: if any element of the HGN test is changed from the approved NHTSA procedure then the VALIDITY of the test is compromised!!!

Video: SFST-What is HGN?

2. Walk & Turn Test

The second field sobriety test is the "*Walk* and *Turn*" (W&T) test. There are two parts to the Walk & Turn test - Balance & Walking.

Prior to taking the test, the officer *should* ask if you have had any injuries or other conditions which might affect your ability to walk or balance as well as any head, back, neck and leg injuries. *An often overlooked medical condition that can cause the classic "unsteadiness" on your feet is vertigo. This condition could be due to problems in the inner ear or even a side effect of some non-prescription medications.*

The *Walk & Turn* test *begins by placing* your left foot on the line. You should be instructed to place your right foot on the line in front of the left foot with your right heel touching against the toe of your left foot *(heel to toe position) with* your arms down at your sides. *The officer should then tell you to maintain this position until you are told to begin the test. Helpful hint – If you start to soon it is* counted against you!

Once you are in the correct position, you will be instructed to take nine heel-to-toe-steps and then turn around and take nine heel-too-toe steps back. *The officer should demonstrate the proper way to take heel to toe steps. Then you should be instructed that on your ninth step to turn on your front foot (Helpful Hint: it should be your left foot) and turn around using several small steps with the other foot. The correct way to perform the turn should then be demonstrated by the officer. Additional instructions include: watch your feet at all times, count the number of steps out loud, once you start walking do not stop until the test is completed. Remember: accurate counting is not one of the standardized clues for this test, however, officers often note this as additional evidence. The last thing the officer should ask you is: "Do you UNDERSTAND the instructions?" If the officer doesn't ask this final question – How can he know that you have heard and understood all of these complicated instructions? This is a great point for an experienced DUI defense attorney to make on cross examination of the officer! The driver must know the rules for the tests. Otherwise, how can his performance be graded?*

The officer is scoring you using the following NHTSA standardized clues for this test. These clues include:

- **Cannot keep balance while listening to instructions**, *actually breaks the starting position*
- **Starts *walking* before instructions are finished**
- **Stops while walking**
- **Does not touch heel-to-toe, *misses by more than ½ inch, actual touching is NOT required***
- **Steps *completely* off the line**
- **Uses arms to balance**
- **Improper turn**
- **Incorrect number of steps**

A failing score on the Walk & Turn test is 2 out of 8 clues. Each clue should be "counted" only once, no matter how many times the clue is present. While performing this test, past clients often talk or critique their performance while actually performing the test! Many times these utterances are noted by the officer and used by him as additional evidence of impairment. Don't be the driver that says, "I can't do this test --- SOBER!" or "I could have done this 3 drinks ago!" Officers and prosecutors love this kind of evidence!

Video: SFST-What is The Walk & Turn Test?

3. One Leg Stand Test

The third test *the officer should administer* is the *"One* Leg Stand" (OLS) test. This test is *one of the "classic tests" that everyone sees suspects trying to perform on the hit TV show "COPS". The officer should tell the driver to stand with their feet together and keep their arms at their sides. The instruction "Don't start the test until told to do so", should be given by the officer. Many people <u>think</u> they know how the officer wants the test performed before they are given the instructions or even given a demonstration of the test. The driver should be told not to sway or hop during the test and to keep his <u>arms</u> by his sides and not raise them in order to keep their balance. <u>Helpful Hint</u>: To be a valid clue – the test subject must raise <u>both arms</u> – not just one! The officer should ask if the driver understands the instructions, so far.*

The instructions for the actual performance portion of the test should now be given. The driver will be asked to stand on either foot and raise the other foot approximately 6 inches off the ground with their toes pointed forward and their foot held parallel to the ground. After giving these complicated instructions, the officer should demonstrate the proper stance for the test. Then, the officer *should tell the driver to count by 1000's until told to stop. One thousand one, one thousand two, one thousand three.......... I think you get the idea, while keeping their foot raised and not putting it down. This test ends when the driver finally has maintained this position for 30 seconds - it is a <u>timed</u> test to 30 seconds. Any clues noticed after 30 seconds have passed should not be scored by the officer.*

The officer should then demonstrate the count and ask if the driver understands the instructions or has any questions. If a driver does in fact have a question, the officer should then answer the question or explain again the portion of the instructions that are confusing the driver.

A <u>challenge</u> to every reader who has only read the instruction portion of the One Leg Stand test <u>once</u> --- <u>get up right now and perform this test!!!!</u>

Did you do any of the following?

- **sway noticeably while trying to balance**
- **put your foot down**
- **hop**
- **<u>raise</u> your <u>arms</u> more than 6 inches from your sides**

These are the 4 standardized clues that are validated for the One Leg Stand test. If the officer believes you showed <u>2</u> out of 4 clues—you <u>fail</u> this test.

Video: SFST- What is The One Leg Stand?

On the 3 tests described so far there are numerous things that can affect a driver's ability to perform the tests satisfactorily on the side of the road including:

-Stimulus not kept 12 to 15 inches from drivers face (HGN)

-Distractions by passing cars or flashing lights (HGN)

- Necessity of a dry and level surface (W&T, OLS)

- 2 inch or higher heels, flip flops or similar footwear (W&T, OLS)

- Driver is 65 years old or older, not necessarily a valid test (W&T, OLS)

-Driver is 50 pounds or more overweight (OLS)

Remember: These are just a few examples of problems that can exist which cause problems for drivers attempting to perform these tests. There are literally dozens of factors that can distract or otherwise affect the driver's ability to perform these tests. I call these tests the "Human Olympics", because it would take an Olympian to be able to perform these tests in the conditions that exist in the real world.

Years ago I had an elderly client that asked the officer that wanted him to perform the SFSTs if he had taken a class on how to administer the SFSTs? The officer said he had and it was a 3 day class. My client was suitably impressed that it took 3 days for the officer to learn how to <u>administer</u> the SFSTs. He then asked the officer if the officer took tests on the SFSTs? Again the officer answered – "yes". He then asked the officer if he got to study for the tests? Again the officer said – "yes – he got to study for the tests". So my client then asked how long would he get to practice/study for the SFSTs? The officer responded – "none". He didn't get to practice the tests. The client told the officer that he didn't think it was fair that the officer took a 3 day class, got to practice giving the SFSTs, got to practice and study for the tests. But the officer wouldn't let him have any time to practice at all. The client then <u>refused</u> to take the SFSTs. In the end the video of the stop and the questions asked by my client were enough to win his DUI case! The lesson learned – Juries like for things to be fair for drivers!

Handheld Breath Test /

Preliminary Breath Test (PBT)

After the SFSTs are administered the officers are trained to confirm the results of the SFSTs are due to the effects of alcohol by using a Preliminary Breath Test device. The PBT testing device should be used to confirm the results of the 3 approved SFSTs. *Outside of training class,* the handheld preliminary breath test (PBT) is often the only "test" used by officers to make the arrest decision in a DUI case! *The PBT is NOT the approved testing device in Georgia. Currently, the only approved testing device is the*

Intoxylizer 5000EN. <u>The numerical results from the handheld PBTs are NOT admissible in court.</u> The officer can only testify to a <u>positive</u> or <u>negative</u> result on the handheld test.

In my experience, many times officers will SKIP one or more (sometimes all of the SFSTs) and ask the driver to submit to the PBT. This is what I call a "Blow and Go" – You take the PBT, get a positive result and then go to jail!!! The driver is asked to simply blow into the box – no other SFST's are given by the officer and with a positive result on the PBT (the officer sees a numerical result such as 0.14 or 0.12) he decides to arrest the driver for DUI. The "Blow and Go" blatantly ignores the officer's extensive training on the proper procedure necessary to conduct a DUI investigation. Remember: there is a reason the PBT test results aren't admissible in court – they are not accurate – PBTs are not approved testing devices/machines in Georgia. They are not accurate and don't have the reliability to accurately measure the alcohol concentration of a drinking drivers breath. The PBT devices are notorious for being unable to distinguish between normal breath and breath that is contaminated by residual mouth alcohol.

Another issue with PBTs is when asked "How long has it been since they consumed alcohol?" many drivers will tell an officer a much longer period of time than it has actually been. They mistakenly believe if they say a "couple of hours" since their last drink, it will convince the officer that they couldn't be "under the influence". In my experience, many times it has only been a couple of minutes since they last took a swallow of beer, mixed drink, breath spray or mouthwash containing alcohol. In this type of situation (and sometimes due to medical conditions like bleeding gums or even dentures) the residual alcohol present in their mouths causes the PBT to give a highly inaccurate reading. Residual mouth alcohol takes up to 20 minutes in a normal and healthy persons' mouth to dissipate - no bleeding gums, dentures, or blood present in their mouth. This is the purpose of the "20 Minute Rule" associated with administering the Intoxilyzer 5000. The "20 minute rule" applies even though the Intoxilyzer 5000 supposedly has a "slope detector" to identify residual mouth alcohol. – Helpful Hint: The officer should ask how long since your last drink? And officer forgets to ask –"Have you used mouthwash, breath spray, etc.?" These often cause a positive result on a PBT.

After seeing this situation repeat itself, literally hundreds of times, I can assure you that the skewed PBT results won't be in your favor. Many times the numerical reading the officer sees will be dramatically higher than the driver's actual alcohol concentration. An example of a false and high reading on a PBT device occurred with a friend of an officer. There was a discussion with the law enforcement officer about the PBT devices lack of a slope detector and the problem with falsely high readings due to the presence of residual mouth alcohol. The officer retrieved his PBT and the person blew into it. The initial reading was NEGATIVE – 0.00. The person then swished a mouthwash containing alcohol in their mouth and spit it out. They talked normally for 5 minutes and a second PBT blow gave a reading of 0.12!!! Which is well above the legal limit in Georgia of 0.08 or as they say "drunk and a half"! The officer said the batteries must be low in the device. He changed the batteries and repeated the same procedure on himself. He first blew a negative result -0.00 - and then after swishing the same mouthwash and spitting it out, talking for 5 minutes – he blew a 0.20 --- 2 ½ TIMES THE LEGAL LIMIT IN GEORGIA!!! These results were due to the inability of the PBT to distinguish between normal breath and breath contaminated with residual mouth alcohol!

Taking SFST With Medical Problems

Remember

- Tell the officer about any injuries to your feet, ankles, legs, knees, hips, back etc. or medical conditions such as vertigo. Anything that can skew the results of the SFST tests must be mentioned.
- You don't have to do any of these SFSTs. You're under no obligation to take any of these field sobriety tests. They are completely voluntary!!!

- Everything you do or say in Phases I, II and III could be used against you. For example, if you say, "I had a glass of wine for dinner," it will be reported that you admitted to drinking.

Let's give an example that happens – all too often - An animal ran out in front of your vehicle, you swerve to avoid it and run into the ditch. It's not a bad accident, but you are shaken up and hit your head and knees when the vehicle plowed into the ditch. You have a bump on your head and a small cut, your head is hurting, and your knees feel tingly and a little weak. Law enforcement is called and soon arrives at the scene of the accident. The officer approaches you and *asks, "would you mind taking some field sobriety tests?"* As *we have* previously discussed, one of the tests *is* the HGN test -- where the officer *moves* his finger or pen Let's give an example that happens – *An animal ran out in front of your vehicle, you swerve to avoid it and run into the ditch. It's not a bad accident, but you are shaken up and hit your head and knees when the vehicle plowed into the ditch. You have a bump on your head and a small cut, your lip is bleeding and you taste blood, your head is hurting, and your knees feel tingly and a little weak. Law enforcement is called and soon arrives at the scene of the accident. The officer approaches you and asks, "would you mind taking some field sobriety test?"* As we have previously discussed, one of the tests is the HGN test – where the officer moves his finger or pen *(the stimulus)* back and forth in front of your face. The officer will tell you to follow the *stimulus* with your eyes without moving your head. *You should immediately tell the officer about how you are feeling as a result of the accident. Headache, cut on your head, lip bleeding, strange feeling in your knees, etc. If you don't make sure the officer knows you have sustained injuries from the accident, the outward manifestations of your injuries may make you* appear intoxicated*. Only you know how the accident has affected you, so you should make it very clear to the officer the extent of your injuries and how they are affecting you.*

The same thing holds true *if you are* subjected to any of the balance tests, such as the *Walk and Turn or the One Leg Stand* tests. If a person has bad ankles, knees, hips, back surgeries, or anything that affects that part of the body, *even if the person is over 65 years old or more than 50 pounds overweight,* it will affect their ability to take these tests and what the results will be. The problem with *the accident* scenario is you *could have a* concussion from *the* accident, *possibly some type of brain damage, blood in your mouth, knee or back injury* or *even* have a *preexisting* condition that would affect *your* ability to complete *the SFSTs*.

Unfortunately, if you don't mention these medical issues immediately the officer won't have all of the facts necessary to make an informed arrest decision, you *could be arrested and transported* to the police station *to be* booked on DUI charges.

I recommend that you always tell the *investigating* officer who is administering any of *the SFSTs* your *specific medical issues,* because *they can become a powerful* defense. *You should be adamant in expressing and explaining your medical conditions.*

If you don't make sure to specifically tell the officer your injuries and how they are affecting you, it will be stated in the *DUI investigation/arrest* report and *in the officers* testimony that you were *unsteady on your feet and swayed during the HGN, failed to maintain your balance on the Walk and Turn, and* you couldn't hold your foot off the ground *in the One Leg Stand.*

If that happens, *the experienced DUI defense* attorney who is representing you can always come back and counter with, "Well, didn't my client tell you that he just *hit his head in the accident / had a cut on his head /injured his knees /* had back surgery, etc? Wouldn't that be a reason he couldn't hold his foot up?" Obviously the answer *should be* "yes", and *the officers' harmful observations and SFSTs results can be logically explained to the jury and any bad inferences prevented.*

Question???? – did anyone catch the references to the busted lip and the taste of blood in the mouth? If the driver had consumed a small amount of alcohol prior to the accident the bleeding lip / taste of blood could cause 2 issues in a DUI case:

1. false high read on the Preliminary Breath Test (PBT)
2. contamination of the subject's mouth with blood contains raw alcohol thereby contaminating the breath sample for the Intox 5000! – (more on the Intox 5000 in the next chapter)

Even this small detail is important so don't forget to tell the officer about this type of issue and make sure your attorney is aware of it! With an experienced and knowledgeable DUI defense attorney this tiny bit of evidence can win a DUI case!

CHAPTER 4 - Intox 5000

The Intoxilyzer 5000 is the current breath-testing machine used in Georgia. Although the device <u>appears</u> to be sophisticated and has the potential for accuracy and reliability, it *is based on 1970's technology! Think about how the Cylons on the original "Battle Star Galactica" television show look antiquated and how outdated that show seems today! The Intox 5000 is nothing more than a machine based on ancient technology and what's worse --- <u>it is</u> a* **computer.** What's especially interesting is that nobody (outside of the manufacturer) has <u>EVER</u> seen the actual programming for that computer. You have to take it on "faith" that it is good and will be accurate in every location it is used, on every individual test subject and in every possible circumstance!

As I've said, the Intox 5000's programming is <u>top secret</u>. When I tell people this <u>fact</u>, nobody wants to believe it. The Georgia Bureau of Investigation (GBI), the FBI, and the Georgia State Patrol (GSP) have <u>never</u> seen it! The computer program language or source code, which governs the operation of the Intox 5000 computer, was formatted by its designers and they set the basic <u>assumptions</u> that determine how the computer is going to operate - using 1970s technology.

With all this being said, the State of Georgia allows law enforcement agencies throughout the state to use the Intoxilyzer 5000 to determine how much alcohol is in your blood by testing a sample of your breath. There are numerous issues that can affect the accuracy of the Intox 5000. These issues fall into two major categories:

1. Officer training and the proper administration of the breath test.
2. The design, calibration, and maintenance of the machine.

Basically - the machine can be affected by human error and the limitations inherent to breath testing devices coupled with the use of 1970s technology.

Officer Training and Proper Administration of Breath Test

In Georgia, potential Intoxilyzer 5000 operators are required to complete a full 2 day training course in order to receive their certificate to operate the Intox 5000. Out of the 2 day course, approximately only <u>3 hours are devoted to the actual operation of the Intox 5000</u> by the trainees. A good portion of this 3 hour period involves learning how to enter into the computer the following information:

- <u>OPERator's LAST NAME</u> = type in last name and any suffix (i.e.: Jr., Sr., III, etc)
- <u>OPERator's FIRST NAME</u> = type in first name (no rank, nickname, or other title)
- <u>OPERator's MIDdle INITial</u> = type in a letter or push enter for none or to skip
- <u>PERMIT NUMBER</u> = type in permit number from Intoxilyzer 5000 permit
- <u>SUBject's LAST NAME</u> = type in last name and any suffix (i.e.: Jr., Sr., III, etc)
- <u>SUBject's FIRST NAME</u> = type in first name (no nicknames, titles, etc)
- <u>SUBject's MIDdle INITial</u> = type in a letter or push enter for none or to skip
- <u>SUBject's Date Of Birth (DOB)</u> = type in date using MM/DD/YY format
- <u>SUBject's DRIVer's LICense</u> = type in two letter code for State and the DL number (i.e.: TN 123456789), if a Georgia (GA) license you may omit the State code. If there is no State Code (i.e.: Military, Foreign, etc) enter DL number. If no drivers license, enter NONE

- <u>ARResting OFFicer's LAST Name</u> = type in last name and any suffix (i.e.: Jr., Sr., III, etc)
- <u>ARResting OFFicer's FIRST Name</u> = type in first name (no rank, nickname, or titles)
- <u>ARResting OFFicer's MIDdle INITial</u> = type in a letter or push enter for none or to skip
- <u>ARResting OFFicer's AGENCY</u> = type in city or county name and agency title (i.e. Decatur P.D. or Fulton Co. S.O.); Georgia State Patrol type in GSP and unit (i.e. GSP Post 4)
- <u>VIOLATION TIME</u> = type in using HHMM format using military time (24 hour clock)
- <u>CASE NUMBER</u> = type in case number, if your agency does not use case numbers, type in citation number or push enter to skip

(The above information is taken directly from the NHTSA Intoxilyzer 5000 Student Training Manual.)

The officers also learn the typical messages that can be displayed from the Intox 5000. Finally the officers learn the limitations <u>inherent</u> with breath alcohol testing. The officers are taught that an operator <u>must</u> concentrate on the <u>quality of the breath sample</u> that is collected by the Intox 5000, <u>the possibility of the sample contamination by residual mouth alcohol</u>, and finally the <u>correlation of the driver's test result compared to the driver's physical condition</u>. Residual mouth alcohol can be a problem if the driver belches, has acid reflux, uses mouthwash or breath freshener spray containing alcohol, has blood present in mouth, has dentures or other dental apparatus or has consumed an alcoholic beverage within a short period of time prior to the Intox 5000 test.

20-Minute Waiting Rule

The State's Intoxilyzer 5000 training manual states in bold print that "all breath tests will be preceded by a twenty (20) minute waiting period" hence the "20-Minute Waiting Rule". Before the

Intox 5000 test is administered, the operator is trained to ensure that the driver has been in a controlled environment and prohibited from consuming any substance containing alcohol. Additionally the driver should be in a location where-if the driver vomits the condition can be noted. Vomiting <u>requires</u> a restart of the 20-minute observation period once the driver has rinsed out his/her mouth with water. In my experience many times the operators don't comply with the 20-minute rule and rush to start the test. This defeats the purpose of the 20-minute, rule which is to eliminate the presence of residual mouth alcohol from the driver's mouth and upper esophagus.

The officer should also look for any type of foreign objects in your mouth which can affect the test results. For example, if you had been dipping tobacco, the little packets of tobacco that you put in your mouth, or if you have blood in your mouth – bleeding gums can easily skew the Intox 5000's test results! If the test was given and you failed it, the defense could prove that tobacco can hold residual amounts of alcohol or the blood present in the subject's mouth could influence the test. Something that also occurs regularly, I often find that the officers fail to inspect a driver's mouth and test drivers that have partial or full sets of <u>dentures</u>! You can imagine the shocked and embarrassed look on an Intoxilyzer Operators face when a client removes his/her dentures <u>in court</u> after the operator testified that he checked the driver's mouth for any foreign objects.

Things That Can Skew Test Results With

The Intox 5000

Many people who have been in court will say they didn't have much to drink and were pulled over and arrested anyway. There are reasons for this to happen and many things that can skew the Intox 5000 test. For example, a person wearing dentures can trap alcohol for 45 minutes and even the adhesive for dentures can contain alcohol. If a driver (who wears dentures) was pulled over and took the Intox 5000 test, dentures can most definitely give a false positive as to the amount of alcohol in your system.

Mouth Contaminants that Skew Test Results

- Tobacco, especially "menthol" flavored
- Dentures and the adhesives used to seal dentures to mouth surfaces
- Mints, lozenges, lip balm, mouthwash or breath sprays that contain, camphor, menthol or SD alcohol
- Blood in a person's mouth from injuries, dental problems, cuts, etc.
- Asthma inhalers which contain alcohol-like volatiles
- Prescriptions with certain ingredients

Unfortunately, Too Common a Scenario

One evening a couple was pulled over to investigate a defective equipment violation (broken tag light) and the officer suspected the female driver had been drinking. They had been physically fighting and the girlfriend had a bloody nose and lip. The officer required her to take a breath test on the Intox 5000. Before administering the Intox 5000, the operator failed to notice the fresh blood and open cuts in her mouth. The test resulted in an extremely high blood alcohol concentration even though there were <u>no physical manifestations</u> of impairment that would be present with such a high blood alcohol content. In other words, she walked and talked normally, when most doctors would say her blood alcohol level [from the skewed test results] would be found in someone that was <u>unconscious</u>!

The Intox 5000 was not designed to give an accurate reading when the operator fails to ensure a <u>non-contaminated breath sample</u> and in this case <u>fresh blood in her mouth</u>. Thank goodness for detailed booking photos that showed an obviously <u>bleeding</u>, <u>bruised</u>, and <u>battered</u> <u>young</u> <u>lady</u> at the time of testing. The machine is <u>not</u> designed to test – <u>blood</u> – <u>only uncontaminated breath</u>. It is not able to accurately test breath that is contaminated with blood.

Design, Calibration and Maintenance of the Intox 5000 Issues

This is not an exhaustive list of the design, calibration, and maintenance issues with the Intox 5000. Entire books have been written and can be written on this subject. I would like to cover a few topics that are of special interest to me.

- Design - The Intox 5000 is nothing more than a machine based on ancient technology from the 1970's. And what's worse --- it is a 1970's computer. What's especially interesting is that nobody has ever seen the actual programming for the Intox 5000's computer. The Intox 5000's programming is <u>top secret</u>. The computer program language or source code, which governs the operation of the Intox 5000 computer, was formatted by its designers and they are responsible for setting the basic assumptions that determine how the computer is going to operate - using 1970's technology.

- Calibration – The Intox 5000 is calibrated when it leaves the manufacturer in Kentucky. Once it enters into operation in Georgia the machine is **never** calibrated until it is taken out of service for some problem or defect and returned to the manufacturer. The State of Georgia has instituted a quarterly inspection procedure for the Intox 5000. The officers responsible for the inspection and certification issue a document certifying that the machine is in good working order. With a machine as complicated as the Intox 5000, it is amazing that the officer can certify it to be in good operating condition when the inspection procedures in Georgia <u>do not require him to even open the machine for internal inspection</u>. Even devices that operate on known scientific principles such as radar are calibrated before and after each shift! However, the document certifying that the Intox 5000 is in good operating condition is actually a simple <u>certificate of inspection and **not** calibration</u>. Remember the Intox 5000 is only <u>calibrated</u> by the <u>manufacturer</u>. If the machine is found to be outside of any working parameters, the State Inspectors are <u>not trained</u> to nor are they capable of calibrating the machine. It <u>must</u> be returned to the <u>manufacturer</u> for maintenance, repair, and recalibration.

The Intoxilyzer 5000 is only calibrated at the 0.08 BAC level. However, in Georgia there are three statutory levels of intoxication that can result in a person being found guilty of DUI. For an average driver of a non-commercial vehicle, the level is 0.08 BAC; for a driver of a commercial vehicle, the level is 0.04 BAC; and for a driver under the age of 21, the level is 0.02 BAC. The problem is the Intox 5000 is only calibrated at 0.08 BAC! An example from my background - as an avid shooting enthusiast - comes from the "sighting" in of the scope on a hunting rifle. Most shooters who "sight in" their rifle scopes at 50 yards would not trust the accuracy of the rifle at 4 times that distance - <u>200 yards</u> - because even being 1 inch off the bulls eye at 50 yards could cause you to <u>miss the entire target at 200 yards</u>!

The Intoxilyzer 5000 being calibrated at 0.08 BAC is being used to prosecute commercial drivers at 0.04 BAC, <u>two times the accuracy</u>, and drivers under age 21 at 0.02 BAC, <u>four times the accuracy</u> than the machine is calibrated for by its manufacturer!

- Maintenance – In order for the Intox 5000 to perform a test, the driver must provide a <u>breath sample</u> of 1.1 liters within three minutes of the test beginning. The flow sensor is responsible for measuring the volume of the breath sample and determining when the 1.1 liter threshold has been met. However, the inspection procedures in Georgia <u>never require this sensor to be inspected and its readings verified</u>. I have had numerous female clients of small stature tell me how they have tried to blow as hard as they could and were not able to provide the sufficient volume of breath required for a valid test. The videos I have viewed of their attempts to provide a sample appear to show them diligently blowing into the machine and still failing to provide the required volume of breath for a valid test. A major suspect that could cause this problem is the flow sensor. Remember, it would only be tested if the machine is taken out of service and sent back to the manufacturer for inspection, repair, and recalibration.

The State of Georgia's reliance on a computer designed using 1970's technology coupled with the inherent issues associated with operator error and a woefully inadequate inspection/certification procedure begs the question - are driver's in Georgia being *persecuted* rather than *prosecuted*?

CHAPTER 5 – What to Expect When You're Accused of DUI

When people are stopped for suspicion of drunken driving, many times they will ask to talk with an <u>attorney</u> before they take any of the field sobriety tests. In Georgia, people do not have that right – and most officers are happy and quick to tell drivers they can't call their attorney.

Another issue which often comes up when I am meeting with clients is the fact that the officer did not read them their <u>Miranda rights</u> when they were pulled over.

The Miranda rights <u>do not apply</u> in Georgia during DUI investigations. The Miranda rights only apply <u>after</u> a person is <u>arrested</u>! After you are arrested then the Miranda rights apply!

After people complete any of the approved States tests, such as the Intox 5000 or blood test, they have a <u>right to an independent test</u> from a qualified person of their own choosing and at their own expense.

For example, if you want a blood test independent from the police testing - and request it, the police officer must accommodate your right to get the blood test. That means the officer will have to take you wherever you want to go, and even to a different hospital / clinic etc. to get the test done. All of this within reason – of course.

Working With Your Attorney

In Georgia, if you are convicted of driving with a blood alcohol content of .08 or above, .04 for commercial drivers, and .02 for drivers under 21 years old, you are automatically considered "per se" guilty of driving under the influence. Even if your driving was not impaired, you are presumed guilty.

Having charges made against you relating to DUI is serious and you need to have an experienced attorney representing you.

Example of a DUI Case

An older experienced commercial truck driver (CDL), was going to lose everything, including his wife, due to a DUI charge.

Prior to the trial, I tried to talk to the officer about possibly reducing the charges and working things out. I explained to the officer that my client had lost his commercial driver's license for months and how this had affected him financially, as well as the imminent end of his marriage. The officer was not convinced. I also explained that he had also been to the DUI school and abstained from driving.

The officer didn't want to cooperate or do anything that would assist my client regarding this situation. I told the officer the only thing we can do is have the trial! The officer's opinion was that it was fine with him, "Win or lose, it didn't matter to him".

As it turned out, I was able to win the case. There were serious issues with the officer's case – incomplete SFSTs, questionable reading of Implied Consent rights, no bad driving on my client's part, etc. The judge heard the case and ruled that the officer had <u>no probable cause to arrest my client in the first place</u>! That means a win for us and makes for an upset and angry officer!

After the Judge's ruling the officer made a snide comment that he hoped my client doesn't kill someone on the highway. The judge responded to the officer that he takes this type of case very seriously, because a drunk driver killed his son! This was shocking news to me and reaffirmed my belief in our Judicial System!

I have found after years of going to court and cross examining officers that one of the quickest ways to get on an officer's bad side and ruin the rest of his day is to point out time and time again how he failed to follow his training and use the proper procedures.

There is a joke about law enforcement and it goes like this.

- There are three things you need to know about law enforcement.

1. They think they are God's gift to women – all women love them!
2. They think they know everything!
3. They don't want to be embarrassed in court!

My response to this joke is, "I can't do anything about Number 1 - God's gift to women, but I can do something about Number 2 and Number 3".

In my profession as an attorney, I generally get along with all law enforcement, but I am still going to do my job – making sure law enforcement did their job <u>correctly</u>!

Even though I am not a certified law enforcement officer, I have had the same training they have had, including the same standardized field sobriety test (SFST) training as a practitioner and as an instructor. Having this experience and training helps me when representing my clients.

Information to Provide

When you meet with an attorney, you need to provide as much information as possible – I have provided a sample client information sheet later in the book for your information. Information you need to provide includes:

1. **Details about what happened**. When you are meeting with your lawyer, you need to give him or her a detailed statement of what happened. This means details as to how much you had to drink, when you started drinking, and when you stopped. Even the details of what you had to eat that day and the last time you ate. Also, you need to mention if there were any open containers with alcohol in the vehicle, etc.

2. **Details of the traffic stop**. You need to bring in the names of any witnesses who may have seen what took place when you were driving and pulled over. Try to remember the events that took place when you were stopped and provide the answers to these questions.

- Do you believe that the traffic stop was video or audio taped?
- What was requested of you when you were pulled over?
- Did you hand the officer your driver's license or your credit card when they asked for your license?
- Did they ask where you were going? We need to know how you answered this question.
- Did you admit that you had been drinking?
- What tests did you perform and how did you do?
- Were you allowed to make any phone calls in the police car or with the officer? If so was it audiotaped?
- Did you refuse to take the states test? If you did refuse to take the states test, your license can be suspended for up to one year.

3. **What was requested of you?** It is important that you remember all of the tests you were required to take, what orders and commands you were given, and how you responded or reacted to each.

Two Types of Courts

When you are charged with DUI, there are two separate courts you will have to go to. They are 1) <u>Administrative License Suspension (ALS) hearing</u> and 2) the actual <u>DUI Criminal Court</u>.

Administrative License Suspension Hearing

In an **Administrative License Suspension Hearing**, the Administrative Law Judge will decide if your license will be suspended. Your license could be suspended for refusing to take the tests, or if there was a .08 BAC alcohol content (or more) in your system.

The appearance before an **Administrative Judge** is completely separate from the DUI hearing. The client does not have to come to the ALS hearing – if they are represented at the ALS hearing by an attorney. The attorney will go to the hearing on behalf of the client – if the driver <u>has</u> foolishly failed to retain a DUI Defense Attorney – the driver <u>must</u> appear at the hearing. I use the ALS procedure as a discovery tool to find out what evidence the state has on the client. The only thing a client is risking at this point is his or her <u>driver's license</u> – not jail time.

Video: ALS-What is an ALS Hearing?

Criminal Trial

When you go to trial for alleged DUI, it is in the criminal court. After you have been arrested, booked and gone through the initial bail process, the first stage of the courtroom proceedings takes place with an **arraignment**.

At the arraignment, the charges against you will be read. The judge will ask if you have an attorney or need the assistance of a court-appointed one. This is the time when the judge will ask if you are entering a <u>plea of guilty or not guilty</u> and if you are requesting a <u>bench or jury trial</u>.

If you are entering a <u>not guilty plea</u> and <u>demand a jury trial</u>, the attorney should file motions and request a motions hearing. The motions hearing is an opportunity for your attorney to get evidence against you suppressed or kept out at the trial. This hearing will be the next hearing and should be held <u>before</u> the actual Jury trial.

At motions hearings, the client is not required to testify, however the choice is a tactical one and is based on the specifics of each case.

While waiting to have the court hearings the prosecution will provide copies of the police reports, videos and any other documents relevant to the case – this is called the "Discovery" process.

Bench Trial vs. Jury Trial

In a criminal case, the client is <u>not required</u> to testify. It is his or her decision. A **bench trial** is the term for trial before a <u>judge</u> rather than a <u>jury</u>. In a bench trial, the <u>judge</u> is the one who will determine all the questions of fact and make the decision of whether or not the driver is <u>guilty</u> or <u>not guilty</u>.

A jury trial involves selecting a group of citizens who will hear the evidence in a case and decide whether the driver is <u>guilty</u> or <u>not guilty</u>. In either case, the defendant is not required to testify.

Which is better a Bench or Jury trial? – this decision is made based on the specific facts of the case, the selected type of defense tactics and the comfort level of the Defendant in testifying at a trial!

Video: Trial-What is the Difference Between A Jury Trial and A Bench Trial?

Conclusion

As you have read through each chapter, you have probably realized the seriousness of a DUI charge. In Georgia, DUI is a criminal offense. You may be facing time in jail, a license suspension, probation, auto insurance rate increase, and a driving record for 10 years with a conviction – and a <u>conviction</u> will remain on your <u>Criminal History</u> for the <u>rest of your life</u>!

Hopefully, you have come to the conclusion from reading this book - the importance of hiring an <u>experienced DUI defense attorney</u> after being pulled over and arrested on DUI charges. Your life and family will be affected if you are <u>convicted</u>. You need to know what to do!

After reading this book, you now know the 3 phases involved in a DUI stop and eventual arrest. Chapter 1 described the initial driving behavior that was observed in Phase I. Phase II described in Chapter 2 educated you on what the officer is looking for when he or she comes into personal contact with you. Your responses, reactions, and physical appearance will play an important part in the officer's assessment of you, and if he or she is going to have you do a field sobriety test.

Taking field sobriety tests can be just what the officer needs to help him decide to arrest you. Phase III the Standardized Field Sobriety Test (SFST) is detailed in Chapter 3, and describes the 3 approved field sobriety tests in Georgia.

You now know the issues with the HGN (Horizontal Gaze Nystagmus), W &T (Walk and Turn) and OLS (One Leg Stand). If the officer decides to arrest you and administers the official state tests, and the results come in with a blood alcohol content of .08 BAC, you will be accused of DUI. (.04 BAC is a commercial driver and .02 BAC if under 21 years of age)

The States tests blood, breath or urine are not necessarily accurate and the results are far from foolproof. The breath test must be calibrated correctly and administered under specific guidelines. There are many things that can alter the results, such as the presence of blood, dentures, tobacco and other contaminates. If you didn't know all of the problems with the States tests <u>before</u> you read this book, you were probably afraid that you had no defense and couldn't possibly win your case!

The good news is - there are experienced DUI Defense Attorneys who can aggressively defend you if you find yourself facing a DUI charge.

If you have been charged with a DUI of alcohol or drugs, based on the breath, blood or urine test, you have a <u>right</u> to defend yourself against these charges! Your DUI Defense Attorney will challenge the officer and prosecutors and make them prove the results of their tests are accurate.

There are many options that you have when facing a DUI charge. The first one is to contact a law firm to represent you and review your case to determine all of the available defenses.

Remember, when you have been arrested for DUI, you only have <u>10 days</u> to protect your driver's license from an ALS suspension. You must act quickly to avoid the serious and life changing repercussions of an ALS driver's license suspension! Please remember, being charged with DUI <u>isn't</u> an automatic conviction and the end of your world - you have a chance to defend yourself with a qualified DUI defense attorney – protect yourself and your family by retaining the best DUI defense attorney that is available to you – ASAP!

About The Author

George F. McCranie IV is a successful and nationally recognized DUI and criminal defense lawyer. George works tirelessly to educate our families, children and friends on criminal defense issues.

George has been seen on countless network television stations, including ABC, CBS, NBC and Fox affiliates around the nation and has also been featured in *USA Today*.

He is also a co-author of the #1 best-selling book "Protect & Defend". In 2012, he was inducted into the "National Academy of Best-Selling Authors" where he was presented with a <u>Golden Quilly Award</u>. George has his 2nd book completed on DUI Defense and anticipates that it will be published in late 2013.

In 1995, George received his Juris Doctor from the Mississippi College School of Law. He completed his Bachelor's degree in History in 1992 from Valdosta State University.

George's legal accomplishments include being named as a Fellow of the Lawyers Foundation of Georgia, an honor that is limited to 4 percent of the attorneys in the State. He is a member of the National College of DUI Defense (NCDD) and a member of the Georgia Association of Criminal Defense Lawyers (GACDL). He is also a former president of the Douglas Bar Association and former member of the Board of Governors of the State Bar of Georgia. He often lectures at area Driver Improvement Schools to better educate the public on DUI laws, and is a National Highway and Safety

Administration (NHTSA) trained instructor for Standardized Field Sobriety Testing.

Although he is based in Coffee County, he serves clients throughout southeast Georgia, and has been practicing law in Georgia since 1996. Between 1996 and 1998, George worked as a criminal prosecutor for the State of Georgia, which has given him experience and insight into how prosecutors handle criminal cases. George has been defending clients against DUI charges since 1998 and understands how the DUI blood tests and breath tests work and how to challenge the results in court.

George has helped many clients deal with all aspects of drunk driving charges that include the following:

- DUI breath tests
- DUI blood tests
- License suspension
- Second-offense DUI
- Commercial driver DUI
- Underage DUI
- Drug-related DUI

George is one of the first attorneys to receive advanced training on Georgia's new Breath Testing device the Intoxilyzer 9000.

Besides continually supporting numerous local charities, George is a Producer of the upcoming documentary film about the Casa Hogar children's home in Acapulco, Mexico which launched production in January of 2013. The documentary will reveal an in-depth look at the incredible story of the Casa Hogar children's home, specifically how the home is providing a nurturing environment with a focus on education in this economically disadvantaged region. This project is important to George and his family as they have seen first-hand the number of young children begging and selling trinkets in the street. The documentary has provided a way for George to assist in helping the needy children of Alcapulco.

Appendix:

Sample Incident Report of a DUI Arrest

			Reporting Agency	
Report Number	Report Date / Time	AM	GEORGIA DEPARTMENT OF PUBLIC SAFETY	
Agency Case Number	Agency CAD Number		Range of Occurrence Date/Time 11:48 PM to 11:48 PM	

One Leg Stand

	Seconds	3 - 10	11 - 20	21 - 30	Crime 4		Notes
Sways		☑	☑	☐			
Raises Arms		☐	☐	☐			
Hops		☐	☐	☐			
Foot Down		☐	☐	☐			

Other Observations

☐ Nystagmus	☐ Eye Lid Tremors	☐ Swaying	☐ Internal Clock	/ 30 Seconds	
☑ PBT ☐ Positive ☐ Negative		Results NONE	Breath Odor STRONG		
Eye Condition BLOODSHOT WATERY	Behavior TALKATIVE		General Appearance DISHEVELED CLOTHING	Speech Pattern SLOW BLURRED	

VEHICLE

State & License Plate Number/Expires GA	VIN	Year	Make	Model	Style	Color
☐ CMV ☐ Hazmat	Registered to					☐ Vehicle Towed

Persons Related to Vehicle

NARRATIVE

On ____, at approximately ____ hours, I observed a ____ traveling eastbound on East ____ Street in ____ County crossing over the fog line back to the center line. As I followed the vehicle further, it turned left onto ____ Street. At that time, I stopped the vehicle and spoke with the ____ driver (____). As, I spoke with ____, I detected a strong odor of alcohol coming from inside the vehicle. I then asked the subject to exit the vehicle. Once ____ stepped out, ____ was somewhat unsteady on ____ feet. ____ then stated ____ had drank a beer earlier. The subject was then asked to blow into my Alco-Sensor box. Subject attempted several times but was unable to. ____ was then asked to perform three field sobriety tests. The results of these tests showed ____ was under the influence of alcohol. ____ was then placed under arrest and read the orange Georgia Implied Consent Card for Subjects Over 21 yrs. of age (Breath). ____ was then transported to the ____ County Jail and given a breath test on the Intoxilyzer 5000. ____ registered a reading of ____ grams. Subject was then charged with D.U.I (Alcohol), Failure to Maintain Lane and Open Container.

DVD-____

EVIDENCE RECORD

Item	Evidence Number	Quantity	Currency Value	Description
		1		

RELATED REPORTS

Report Name	Report Number / Description
Uniform Traffic Citation	
Uniform Traffic Citation	
Uniform Traffic Citation	

REPORTING OFFICER / SUPERVISOR APPROVAL

Reporting Officer			Approving Supervisor	
	Rank		ID Number Rank SERGEANT	
Signature			Signature	

Implied Consent Notice

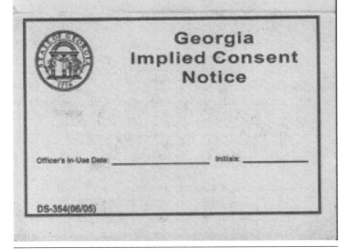

IMPLIED CONSENT NOTICE / SUSPECTS UNDER AGE 21

Georgia law requires you to submit to state administered chemical tests of your blood, breath, urine, or other bodily substances for the purpose of determining if you are under the influence of alcohol or drugs.

If you refuse this testing, your Georgia driver's license or privilege to drive on the highways of this state will be suspended for a minimum period of one year. Your refusal to submit to the required testing may be offered into evidence against you at trial.

If you submit to testing and the results indicate an alcohol concentration of 0.02 grams or more, your Georgia driver's license or privilege to drive on the highways of this state may be suspended for a minimum period of one year.

After first submitting to the required state tests, you are entitled to additional chemical tests of your blood, breath, urine or other bodily substances at your own expense and from qualified personnel of your own choosing.

Will you submit to the state administered chemical tests of your (designate which tests) under the implied consent law?

Georgia
Implied Consent
Notice

Officer's In-Use Date: _____   Initials: _____

DS-354(06/05)

Intoxilyzer 5000 Invalid Sample Print Out

"INSUFFICIENT SAMPLE"

If the subject fails to provide an adequate breath sample within the allotted three minute sampling time, for either breath sample, the instrument will print "INSUFFICIENT SAMPLE" for that breath sample. This result is *not* an admissible test result. Instruct subject how to provide breath sample and retest. (See page 53 Komala v. State.)

TEST	G/210L	TIME
DIAGNOSTICS	OK	08:20EDT
AIR BLANK	.000	08:20EDT
*SUBJECT SAMPLE	---	08:24EDT
AIR BLANK	.000	08:24EDT
* INSUFFICIENT SAMPLE		

OR

TEST	G/210L	TIME
DIAGNOSTICS	OK	10:10EDT
AIR BLANK	.000	10:10EDT
SUBJECT SAMPLE	.034	10:12EDT
AIR BLANK	.000	10:12EDT
DIAGNOSTICS	OK	10:14EDT
AIR BLANK	.000	10:14EDT
*SUBJECT SAMPLE	---	10:17EDT
AIR BLANK	.000	10:18EDT
*INSUFFICIENT SAMPLE		

Intoxilyzer 5000 enhanced version (serial # >10000) will also print the Breath Volume of the last attempt. This is not an alcohol concentration and is not an adequate sample.

TEST	G/210L	TIME
DIAGNOSTICS	OK	08:20EDT
AIR BLANK	.000	08:20EDT
*SUBJECT SAMPLE	---	08:24EDT
BREATH VOLUME 0.425 LITERS		
AIR BLANK	.000	08:24EDT
*INSUFFICIENT SAMPLE		

OR

TEST	G/210L	TIME
DIAGNOSTICS	OK	10:10EDT
AIR BLANK	.000	10:10EDT
SUBJECT SAMPLE	.034	10:12EDT
AIR BLANK	.000	10:12EDT
DIAGNOSTICS	OK	10:14EDT
AIR BLANK	.000	10:14EDT
*SUBJECT SAMPLE	---	10:17EDT
BREATH VOLUME 0.355 LITERS		
AIR BLANK	.000	10:18EDT
*INSUFFICIENT SAMPLE		

Department Of Driver Services 1205 Form

GEORGIA DEPARTMENT OF DRIVER SERVICES

ATTACH DRIVERS LICENSE HERE

P.O. BOX 80447 / CONYERS, GEORGIA 30013

SWORN REPORT OF THE ARRESTING OFFICER: ADMINISTRATIVE LICENSE SUSPENSION AND IMPLIED CONSENT

TYPE OR PRINT CLEARLY (IN INK) ALL REQUESTED INFORMATION

INCIDENT DATA

INCIDENT DATE: MM/DD/YR	INCIDENT TIME: AM PM	COUNTY OF OCCURRENCE:	ROAD OF OCCURRENCE:	DIRECTION & DISTANCE FROM & NAME OF NEAREST TOWN:
DUI CITATION NUMBER ONLY:	COMMERCIAL VEHICLE: YES _____ NO _____		HAZARDOUS MATERIALS PRESENT: YES _____ NO _____	

DRIVER DATA

NAME: LAST	FIRST	MIDDLE	DATE OF BIRTH: MM/DD/YR
CURRENT ADDRESS (STREET, CITY, STATE, ZIP CODE):			

DRIVERS LICENSE NUMBER:	STATE OF ISSUE:	LICENSE CLASS:	LICENSE RESTRICTIONS:	HEIGHT:	WEIGHT:	SEX: ___MALE ___FEMALE

SWORN REPORT, ARRESTING OFFICER DATA, AND TEST DATA

ARRESTING OFFICER'S NAME: LAST FIRST MIDDLE	AVO TELEPHONE NO:	ARRESTING OFFICER'S PRECINCT, ZONE, OR POST ASSIGNMENT:
NAME OF LAW ENFORCEMENT AGENCY REPRESENTED BY ARRESTING OFFICER:		BADGE #:
LAW ENFORCEMENT AGENCY MAILING ADDRESS (STREET, CITY, AND ZIP CODE)		AGENCY'S ORI NUMBER:
TEST RESULTS: GRAMS	INSTRUMENT SERIAL NUMBER: OPERATOR'S NAME:	OPERATOR PERMIT NO:

This arresting officer swears or affirms that at the date and time noted above, the arresting officer, having reasonable grounds to believe that the driver had been driving or in actual physical control of a moving motor vehicle while under the influence of alcohol or a controlled substance, lawfully arrested the driver for violating O.C.G.A. 40-6-391; or that the driver was involved in a motor vehicle accident or collision that resulted in serious injury or fatality.

MARK ONE ONLY: The driver was requested to submit to state administered chemical testing as required by law and:

_____ The driver refused to submit to the designated state administered chemical testing; or

_____ Chemical test results indicated an alcohol concentration of 0.08 grams or more; or

_____ The driver was under the age of 21 and the chemical tests results indicated and alcohol concentration of 0.02 grams or more; or

_____ The driver was operating a moving commercial motor vehicle and the chemical tests results indicated an alcohol concentration of 0.04 grams or more.

The arresting officer's signature constitutes certification that the arresting officer delivered a copy of this form to the driver.

Sworn and Subscribed to me this _____ day of _____, 20____

_____
Arresting Officer's Signature   Report Date

_____
Notary Public

NOTE: PERSONALLY GIVE YELLOW COPY TO LICENSEE

OFFICIAL NOTICE OF INTENT TO SUSPEND

You are hereby served Official Notice of the Suspension of your drivers license and/or your privilege to operate a motor vehicle for a period to be determined by the Department of Driver Services. If you refuse chemical testing, your license will be suspended for one year. Your suspension will begin at midnight on the 30th day following the date of arrest for the reason checked above. Hearing procedures are on the reverse side of the Driver's copy.

TEMPORARY DRIVING PERMIT

This is a valid temporary driving permit for a period of (30) days from the incident date above if signed by the arresting officer. **This is not a temporary driving permit if the driver's license or privilege is suspended, cancelled or revoked or driver is unlicensed.**

NOTE TO OFFICER: The reason for non-issuance of this permit must be stated on this form and the driver must receive a copy of this "Notice" to meet the requirements as stated in O.C.G.A. 40-5-67.1. **TEMPORARY LICENSE MUST BE SIGNED IF DRIVER WAS VALID AT THE TIME OF ARREST.**

___Yes	___No	License surrendered? If No, state the reason.
___Yes	___No	Is the surrendered license attached on the upper left corner of the DDS copy of this report?
___Yes	___No	Is the surrendered license a *Habitual Violator Probationary* license?

Signature of Driver: _____

Signature of Arresting Officer: _____

SIGN TO VALIDATE TEMPORARY DRIVING PERMIT

Department of Driver Services Copy

DS 1205 (Rev. 04/06)

Forms B-5

Office of State Administrative Hearings

Helpful Information to Know

Office of State Administrative Hearings

What is OSAH (Office of State Administrative Hearings)?

The Office of State Administrative Hearings (OSAH) is an agency created by statute and empowered to conduct the initial or final hearing in contested cases for a number of other state agencies. For a determination of those state agencies who are required to utilize OSAH for the conduct of their initial hearings, and examination of O.C.G.A. 50-13-2(1) and 42 is required. Any other state agency is authorized to contract with OSAH for the conduct of initial hearings. In addition, a state agency may provide by statute or rule for OSAH to conduct final hearings on the agency's behalf.

DUI Rights Cards

Admit Nothing • Deny Everything • Demand Proof ℠

George F. McCranie, IV
Attorney at Law

Website: www.mccranielawfirm.com
Website: www.beatagadui.com
E-mail: georgemccranie@mccranielawfirm.com

301 E. Jackson Street • Douglas, GA 31533
Phone: 912-383-7581 • Fax: 912-383-7583

Know Your Constitutional Rights & Use Them:

1. You have the right to REMAIN silent even before you are arrested. Anything you say or do (such as roadside sobriety evaluations) CAN and WILL BE USED AGAINST you.

2. You have a right to consult privately with an attorney, and if you request to exercise this valuable right, all interrogation must stop and no police officer can question you further, REMAIN silent. Call **912-383-7581** collect.

3. Assume that every word you speak -- in a police station, police car, to a jail inmate or in a jail cell is being RECORDED. It probably is! REMAIN SILENT! Only talk to your attorney.

DUI Questionnaire

NAME:

ADDRESS:

EMPLOYER:

HOME PHONE:

CELL PHONE:

SOC. SEC. NO:

DATE OF BIRTH:

DRIVERS LICENSE NO:

STATE:

Please answer the following questions to the best of your knowledge; doing so will enable us to provide the best possible defense for your case.

1. How much had you had to drink in the 24 hours prior to your arrest?

_____

_____

_____

2. When and where did you consume the alcohol? Who witnessed the amount of alcohol you consumed?

_____

_____

_____

_____

3. Please state the route driven before your arrest:

_____

_____

_____

_____

4. If you were pulled over at a roadblock, please give detailed information about all the circumstances of your driving conduct when you approached the roadblock.

_____

_____

_____

_____

5. Please describe the vehicle you were driving at the time of your arrest (i.e. make, model, out-of-state tag). Was it in good working condition?

_____

_____

_____

_____

6. How long did the officer follow you or was in visual contact with you prior to the blue lights being turned on?

_____

_____

_____

_____

7. What was the first statement or comment made to you by the police officer?

_____

_____

_____

_____

_____

_____

_____

8. Please give a description of the conversations you had with the officer before and after the arrest.

_____

_____

_____

_____

_____

_____

_____

_____

_____

_____

_____

_____

_____

9. Please describe any types of test you were given by the road (walk, run, flying eagle, ABC's). What about test given at the jail?

_____

_____

_____

_____

_____

_____

10. What was the reason you were arrested at the very beginning?

Circle One: Accident, roadblock, pulled over, other

Describe why.

_____

_____

_____

_____

_____

_____

_____

_____

Were you handcuffed? _____yes _____no   if so, were they in front or back? _____

Were you searched?   _____yes _____no

Were you asked questions concerning medications or health problems?

_____

_____

Where were you taken?

_____

_____

Who questioned or interviewed you?

_____

_____

11. Were you given an implied consent warning? This may not have been given to you until you were under arrest or placed in handcuffs or in the back of the police vehicle. Did you sign any forms on the roadway or at the police station electing whether or not to consent to having a chemical sobriety test made?

_____

_____

_____

_____

_____

_____

12. Were you read your Miranda rights? _____yes
_____no

13. Did you request independent testing? _____yes
_____no

14. How long were you kept without access to a
phone?_____

15. Did you request the assistance of an attorney and access to a
phone to call an
attorney? _____yes _____no

16. Who helped you obtain release from jail? (Name, Address,
Phone No.):

_____

_____

_____

_____

_____

17. What was the method of bonding out of jail? (Own recognizance,
cash bond, etc.)

_____

_____

_____

18. What other people were present at the jail during your arrest?

_____

_____

_____

_____

_____

19. Which towing company removed your vehicle from the roadway? Or did they allow someone to come and get the car?

_____

_____

_____

20. What kind of tests were you required to take at the police station? Where and how were the tests performed? Were there other people present? How much time did the officer wait before requesting the test? Did the person that administered your test show any type of certification or proof that they were authorized to run that particular type of test (blood, urine, or other test)? Did you see video cameras? If yes, where?

_____

_____

_____

_____

_____

_____

_____

_____

_____

21. Were you required to take a breath test? If so, what did you register and how many times did they require you to blow? Did you belch, hiccup, cough, vomit, etc., before or during the tests?

_____

_____

_____

_____

_____

_____

_____

_____

22. To the best of your ability, in the space provided below, please draw the room where the breath test was taken. Please include the location of any equipment in the room, such as videotape equipment, radio equipment, etc.

23. Were you requested to take a urine test?   _____yes _____no

24. Were you requested to take a blood test?   _____yes _____no

If so, which facility was used to draw blood?_____

Was the person who drew blood a doctor or nurse?_____

Were you required to sign any documents?_____

Was your arm swabbed with an alcohol base or a Betadine solution? _____

25. When, if ever, did you make it known to the police that you wanted an attorney?

_____

_____

_____

_____

26. Did you receive the Form 1205 informing you of an Administrative License Suspension?

_____yes _____no

27. What comments, if any, did the officer make regarding the fact that your license was going to be suspended?

_____

_____

_____

_____

_____

28. Please check yes if you currently do or ever have suffered from any of the following:

Problems with the inner ear labyrinth? Yes___ No___

Influenza (flu)? Yes___ No___

Strep Infection? Yes___ No___

Vertigo (Dizziness)? Yes___ No___

Measles? Yes___ No___

Syphilis? Yes ___ No___

Muscular Dystrophy? Yes__ No__

Multiple Sclerosis? Yes__ No __

Korchaff's syndrome? Yes__ No__

Brain hemorrhage? Yes__ No__

Epilepsy? Yes__ No__

Hypertension? Yes__ No__

Glaucoma? Yes__ No__

Dentures? Yes__ No__

Partials? Yes__ No__

Bonded or Capped teeth? Yes__ No__

Broken teeth? Yes__ No__

Pitted or Deep Cavities in teeth? Yes__ No__

Bleeding gums? Yes__ No__

Open Wounds in mouth? Yes__ No__

29. Prior to the arrest did you have any changes in atmospheric pressure? Yes__ No__

30. Had you consumed an excessive amount of caffeine before being stopped by the officer? Yes__ No__

31. Had you been exposed to an excessive amount of nicotine? Yes__ No__

32. Before being arrested did you consume any prescription drugs? Yes ___ No___

If yes, what?

_____

Frequently Asked Questions

Question:

What does an officer look for before pulling a person over for a suspected DUI?

Answer:

An officer will look for a driver who is weaving, doesn't stay in his or her lane, makes wide turns, has slow responses to traffic signals and is driving into opposing traffic. Driving too slow is also a red flag. Driving 10 miles below the speed limit will catch an officer's attention.

Question:

Should I take a field sobriety test on the side of the road if I am stopped?

Answer:

No. In most instances, these tests are difficult for many people to conduct when they are sober. The HGN test is not conclusive since there are over 44 other causes to HGN (Nystagmus). This test is only as good as the officer's ability to follow the testing procedures properly.

Question:

How long does a DUI conviction stay on a person's record?

Answer:

A DUI conviction is considered a criminal offense. Georgia's laws allows a DUI offense to be viewed for 10 years. However, it will stay on your criminal record for the rest of your life.

Question:

I received a temporary driver's license after I was arrested, as well as tickets. What does that mean?

Answer:

The temporary driver's license is a 30-day driving permit. You have 10 days to write a letter requesting a hearing on your case and must include a $150.00 check or money order. If you do not follow through requesting a hearing within the 10 days, your license will be suspended 30 days from the date of your arrest. This suspension can be from 1-5 years.

Question:

What is a pre-trial and plea negotiation conference?

Answer:

This is an attempt to work out the best disposition for your case between your attorney and the prosecutor. Many times this is not resolved until the eve of the trial.

Question:

How long will it take to resolve my case?

Answer:

An experienced attorney knows what it takes to get good results. A case can last anywhere from a few months to a year. A case that goes to trial can take longer. Much is dependent on what the facts and circumstances are of your case and the desired outcome.

Question:

What are the penalties for DUI in Georgia?

Answer:

The penalties in Georgia are severe. A DUI conviction will bring criminal charges, fines, penalties, and jail time. It will also adversely affect your insurance rates and employment, not to mention your family.

Consequences of A DUI Conviction

GEORGIA DUI PENALTIES

.

First Offense Within a Five Year Period

Fine

$300.00 -$1000.00 plus any statutory surcharges (typically 15-25%).

Jail

10 days to 12 months, all except for 24 hours may be suspended, stayed or probated.

Theoretically, if your blood alcohol level is less than 0.08 grams %, you do not even have to do the 24 hours. Practically speaking, don't count on it. Moreover, on all DUI cases made on or after May 1, 1999, if you plead guilty or are convicted of DUI, you must be placed on twelve months probation less any jail time received.

Community Service

The law requires a minimum of 40 hours of community service unless you are under 21 years of age in which case you must do at least 20 hours. The actual time is set by the Court.

License Suspension

If you are 21 or over, your license will be suspended for one year. You will be able to get your license back at the end of 120* days if you have completed an alcohol/drug risk reduction course (DUI school) and paid the appropriate reinstatement fee. During those 120 days, you will be able to get a limited driving permit.

If you are under 21, your license will be revoked for either 6 months (under 0.08 blood alcohol level) or 12 months (0.08 or higher) and no limited permit is allowed.

*If you are convicted of a DUI charge that involves drugs, your Georgia driver's license or privilege to drive in Georgia will be suspended for one year, and you will not be able to get it reinstated for six months. No limited driving permit is allowed.

Second Offense Within a Five Year Period

Fine

$600-$1000 plus any statutory surcharges.

Jail

90 days to 12 months, all except three days of which may be suspended, stayed, or probated. As with a first DUI within a five year period, for any case made on or after May 1, 1999, you must do twelve months probation less any jail time.

Community Service

For cases made on or after July 1, 2001, the minimum community service is thirty days.

License Suspension

Cases Made On or After July 1, 2001

Just when you thought you had it all figured out, the 2001 Georgia Legislature passed House Bill 385. Like the prior law, for cases made on or after July 1, 2001, the driver's license of anyone convicted of a second DUI within a five year period will be suspended for three years. However, unlike prior law, you will not be able to have your driver's license reinstated **for a period of 18 months**. The first twelve months is a hard suspension with no limited permit or hardship license. After that, an ignition interlock limited permit is required for 6 months. It appears that the judge can no longer order no driving for the full term of suspension as he/she could under prior law.

Under the current law, for a second or subsequent conviction within a five year period, an ignition interlock device must be installed on all vehicles registered to the offender unless the court notifies the Department of Public Safety of exemptions for multiple vehicles due to hardship.

Effect on Those Under 21 Years of Age

A cursory reading of the new statute appears to allow those under 21 who are convicted of a second in five year DUI to have their driver's license reinstated after just one year. However, a more thorough reading reveals that these underage drivers are subject to Code Section 40-5-63 (See revised Code Section 40-5-57.1 of House Bill 385). Section 40-5-63 requires an 18 month suspension for second in five DUI convictions.

License Plates

Brand new to a second conviction is license plate confiscation. Under the 2001 legislation, for cases made on or after July 1, 2001, upon conviction, the license plates of all vehicles registered to the offender will be confiscated. No new plates will be issued to the offender until such time as he/she obtains a limited permit or full reinstatement of driving privileges. Under certain conditions, a hardship license plate is available to a co-owner of the vehicle or to family members.

Photo Published

On cases made on or after May 1, 1999, your photograph, name and address, as well as the date, time, place of arrest will be published in your local newspaper. You will be charged $25.00 for this notice.

THIRD Offense Within a Five Year Period

Fine

$1000-$5000 plus statutory surcharges.

Jail

120 days to 12 months, all but 15 days of which may be suspended, stayed or probated. As with a first or second DUI within a five year period, for any case made on or after May 1, 1999, you must do twelve months probation less any jail time you are sentenced to.

Community Service

For cases made on or after July 1, 2001, you must do 30 days of community service.

License Revocation

If you are 21 or over, you have achieved the status of Habitual Violator and your license is revoked for five years. For cases made on or after May 1, 2000, in order to get your probationary license after two years, you will have to complete DUI school, complete assessment and counseling, and have the **ignition interlock device** installed in your car. You can then get your probationary license and will be required to have the ignition interlock device for at least six months.

As stated above in the section for second in five DUI convictions, it appears that, pursuant to Code Section 40-5-63 (See revised Code Section 40-5-57.1) those under age 21 also will suffer the same five year suspension.

Alcohol Assessment and Treatment

You must be evaluated and complete all treatment recommendations before you can get your ignition interlock permit.

License Plate Confiscation

As for a second DUI conviction in a five year period, the license plates of all motor vehicles registered to the offender must be surrendered. On or after July 1, 2001, once the offender obtains either a probationary license or full reinstatement, license plates can be reissued for the offender's vehicles. Special hardship plates are available in certain circumstances for co-owners or family members.

Photo Published

Your photograph, name and address, as well as the date, time, place of arrest will be published in your local newspaper. You will be charged $25.00 for this notice.

What Our Clients Are Saying

August 2011 - I lost weight, sleep and nearly lost my family worrying about my case. George saved me and I wish I would have hired him sooner. - T. P.

February 2011 - Mr. McCranie represented me in a DUI charge, he saved me thousands of dollars on my insurance costs and my job! George was the best investment I ever made. - J. R.

January 2012 - My daughter was in a wreck, resulting in some charges. I knew George from our home town and I knew if he couldn't help us, he would advise me who could. George and his staff made this terrible ordeal a lot easier to deal with. They not only advised, but listened to my concerns as a mother. I would highly recommend them to any and every one seeking legal counsel. Thank you all so very much. - E. M.

JANUARY 2012 - MY EXPERIENCE WAS GREAT. ALL MY QUESTIONS WERE ANSWERED PROMPTLY AND THE PROCESS WAS EXPLAINED TO ME IN DETAIL. JENNIFER IN THE OFFICE WAS ALWAYS WONDERFUL. GEORGE IS VERY KNOWLEDGEABLE AND DOES AN EXCELLENT JOB. I WOULD RECOMMEND THIS FIRM TO EVERYBODY. THANKS FOR

April 2012 - I thought George did all he could to obtain the best results in my cases. I had several DUI charges pending at one time and was facing extensive jail time. Thanks to George I was not sentenced to jail. - T. B.

May 2012-I would recommend everyone to hire Mr. George for any legal problem; he is a very professional and respected lawyer. I am very satisfied with his work and would recommend George to everyone. –D.S.

MAY 2012- WE WERE ALWAYS GREETED WITH FRIENDLY AND COURTEOUS STAFF, AND NEVER HAD TO WAIT LONG AT ALL. GEORGE ALWAYS EXPLAINED EVERYTHING SO WE COULD UNDERSTAND WHICH WE NEEDED BECAUSE THIS WAS OUR FIRST AND HOPEFULLY LAST TIME NEEDING LEGAL HELP. WE WERE VERY IMPRESSED WITH GEORGE AND THE OFFICE STAFF. WE WILL MOST DEFINITELY RECOMMEND YOU TO OTHERS. – D. L.

August 2011 – Great experience with McCranie Law Firm. I am Pleased with the outcome of my case. – A. M.

MAY 2012- I AM THANKFUL FOR HIS SERVICES AND WOULD DEFINITELY REFER HIM TO ANYONE ELSE IN NEED OF LEGAL REPRESENTATION. – L.D.

April 2012 – I could not have made a better choice. My son had said to me long before I needed representation that if I ever needed a lawyer I was to call George McCranie. I did and I am very pleased, extremely pleased with the end result. – M. V.

September 2011 – I was unsure about hiring an attorney to represent me. After discussing the issues of my case with Mr. McCranie I realized a DUI was more serious than I had first thought. George saved me thousands of dollars in insurance as well as lost wages. – D. S.

February 2012 – I was charged with aggravated stalking. Thanks to Mr. McCranie's hard work the charges against me were dismissed. George saved my life. – P. B.

DECEMBER 2011 – GEORGE REPRESENTED ME IN A PERSONAL INJURY CASE AND I WAS VERY PLEASED WITH THE RESULTS. GEORGE AND HIS STAFF STAYED LATE TO MEET WITH ME AND WERE ALWAYS HELPFUL AND COURTEOUS. – J. R.

Made in the USA
Charleston, SC
09 July 2013